A SAMPLING OF LIFE

ONE TASTE AT A TIME

a food memoir

love
Martha Wallace

SWALLOW
PUBLISHING

About the Author

Martha McCray Wallace was born in Cleveland Ohio, and currently resides in Clarkston, Georgia. A self-described contented mother of five heartbeats and Nana of eight grandangels, Martha is the recipient of the 2013 Helen Friese/Village Writers Award for her poem Will's House. She graduated from Georgia Perimeter College where she majored in journalism.

Seeking to continue to perfect her writing skills, she attended and graduated from Agnes Scott College in Decatur, Georgia and won the Janet Newman Preston Creative Writing Prize for Nonfiction in 2015 as well as had several poems published in Nandi Magazine.

Table of Contents

Part III: The International Epicurean

A Second Serving:
Sharing the Gift of Food from Family and Friends

— III —

Final Thoughts

Palatable Pointers

"Memorable meals shared with family or friends is another page in the tapestry of your life to be treasured."
– Martha Wallace

"Cooking is like love. It should be entered into with abandon, or not at all."
– Harriet Van Horne

"You learn to cook so that you don't have to be a slave to recipes. You get what's in season and you know what to do with it."
– Julia Child

"What I've enjoyed most, though, is meeting people who have a real interest in food and sharing ideas with them. Good food is a global thing and I find that there is always something new and amazing to learn—I love it!"
– Jamie Oliver

"If you really want to make a friend, go to someone's house and eat with him... the people who give you their food give you their heart."
– Cesar Chavez

"The best comfort food will always be greens, cornbread, and fried chicken."
– Maya Angelou

It's difficult to think anything but pleasant thoughts while eating a homegrown tomato.
– Lewis Grizzard

Acknowledgments

I wish to personally thank the following people for being an inspiration and their contributions to my knowledge and other help in creating this book:

First to God above, then those who continue to live bravely and lovingly in my mind: my dearest grandpa, Willie Thomas Jr., who taught me the wonders of coaxing God's bounty from this beautiful earth, and my grandmother, Corine Thomas; my mother, Aleta McCray, whose heart continues to beat through mine, and dad Casey McCray. To my lifelong ride-or-die chick, Gwen Scales (Lucinda); to Sheila Booker, who taught me about getting the most out of technology—beautiful spirits, gone but never forgotten.

While attending college I carried the spirits of my mother and grandmother to each class, campus, and continent that I was blessed to step upon. Also to the memory of Minister Pamela Bryant, who lovingly taught me about the tentmaker's job and blessed so many young lives through her ministry.

To my Uncle Robert and Aunt Renee Lawrence (whom we recently lost), who believed in my abilities even when I had no idea that I doubted I had the mental strength to return to school at an age when many of my friends were considering retirement. I did it, Uncle, Auntie—Magna Cum Laude!

To my five heartbeats without whom the story would have many blank pages. To all of my grandchildren who are a constant spring of inspiration. Your Nana rocks and raises the bar! To my siblings... portions of our earlier lives slide through the pages of this memoir. You may not remember everything as I am older than you, but this is told as I best remember it. Love you always, Henry, may you rest in heavenly peace, Tony, Karen, William, Vernon, LaWanda, and Lucky.

*A special dedication to Tony, my Tone-Tone. We love and miss you, brother dear.

To Carolyn Cochran, "Peaches" Lougayne Johnson, Jessie and Alicia Bonds, and Ruth Heard, my elegant, charming Cleveland connection. We have shared many wonderful occasions as well as supported each other when things got rough. My arms are around you and those you also hold dear.

To my ATL connection: My TRIO Student Services Support Family at Georgia Perimeter College; Neely "Bee" Terrell, you are blessed and always a blessing to so many. To Jazzmin, Sarah, and my Scottie and Witkaze Sisters of Agnes Scott College. To Devaill, my mentee who fell in love with my first words and encouraged me to share these gifts to all. To each and every professor from Georgia Perimeter College, to the amazing Agnes Scott College family (you know who you are, I love you) that challenged me, guided me and pushed me, encouraged and believed in me. To Dean Christine Cozzens, who first told me that I was indeed an exceptional writer.

Bon Appetit!

Part I
Taste of Earlier Times

Growing in Will's Garden

As a child, I was fortunate enough to be able to spend lots of time with my grandparents. My mother's parents, Will and Corine.

One early summer morning, I went out the back door while my grandfather was clearing away the breakfast dishes and Granny was making the beds. We had enjoyed hot buttery cheese grits, scrambled eggs, bacon, chunks of ham, and grandpa's open-faced cheese toast. He put the bread (different types—English muffins, wheat slices, white slices, and sometimes raisin bread), slathered with soft sweet butter and topped with a piece of Colby longhorn cheese, under the oven broiler to melt. The English muffins had peaks that got golden brown, and the crannies cradled the cheese. The wheat and white bread absorbed the butter and cheese like a sponge, producing soggy, gooey goodness. The raisins plumped up and drank in the cinnamon and sugar that had been dusted on top. The kitchen smelled like a bakery.

For as long as I could remember, my grandparents had a small silver coffee percolator with a glass bubble in the top that the coffee kissed as it percolated. The bloop-bloop sound of the coffee maker and the smell of freshly brewed coffee was my alarm clock. In the morning, early before sunrise, I could hear the tapping of Grandpa's shoes on the linoleum as he listened to the southern gospel music pouring from the brown radio on the kitchen counter with the big round dial that looked like a giant eye. It had a tortoiseshell covering with golden numbers around it. Grandpa turned it on as soon as he went into the kitchen. The kitchen was soon filled with good smells and sounds.

My grandfather Will always had a garden and rarely bought produce from the grocery store. Raised as an Alabama sharecropper, he knew how to coax good things to eat from the earth. I was told he worked long and hard in cotton fields of the South, and when he moved north the steel mills took their place. I tried to visualize him in those places, but I couldn't get past the gentle, quiet man with the soft, light-brown eyes tenderly caring for tender vegetables, weeding, humming, watering, and humming. Each morning after breakfast he would survey the garden; what is ripe, always ripe, not doing well. He collected vegetables, such as beets, collard greens, green onions, garlic, tomatoes, and cucumbers and brought them in the house and placed them next to the sink, where we would wash the dirt off and store in the appropriate place. He also loved flowers; he had several plastic white ducks lined up on either side of the front steps to the porch, filled with plants. Vivid red geraniums, yellow black-eyed Susans, and red, tangerine, and golden marigolds greeted visitors. Concord grape vines invaded spots, threading through the chain link fence surrounding the side of the house and backyard, providing a sweet and tasty treat any time of day. Purple and pink petunias fluttered along the driveway, with patches of spearmint standing tall behind them.

My grandmother, Corine, worked in a hospital, and I was excited each day when we went to pick her up from work. I sat in the front seat, turning the dials on the car radio trying to find a song I knew. Grandpa loved country and western music, and there were plenty of ballads to accompany us as we headed to pick her up.

If Grandpa was the breakfast king, she was the dinner queen. On any given Sunday, Granny would pop a plump capon with cornbread dressing in the oven, roasting it until it was golden brown. I stood nearby watching her as she washed fresh turnip greens and chopped the roots to cook. She had a special blackened cast iron skillet just to make her delicious cornbread in. Once it was done and had "sweated," she turned it out on a plate and I sliced and buttered it. We washed and sliced tomatoes and cucumbers from the garden and placed them in a little vinegar with salt and pepper. These fresh garden treasures accompanied the greens, as well as hot baked sweet potatoes with butter (she added cinnamon, and brown sugar for us younger ones) melting inside. It is fair to say that this contributed to my love for cooking. The meals were simple to many, but they were good, healthy meals that we all enjoyed.

Chow-Chow Down

Granny wasn't much of a "dig in dirt" garden girl; she left that to Grandpa. She was a domestic goddess who kept a spic-and-span clean house, beds made with hospital corners, and her white sheets waved in the breeze on her clotheslines out in the backyard, held in place by wooden clothespins. She preferred hanging her linen outside—she said the sun would whiten the sheets and the fresh air would freshen them.

There was one thing, however, that she produced in the kitchen that was distinctly her undertaking, her project, "Chow-Chow." Chow-chow was a type of relish that she made every couple of years and stored in shiny Mason jars in the basement dark room under the porch.

Grandpa would bring Granny's old four-gallon stoneware canning crock from its shadowy hiding place, take it out to the backyard, and give it a good shower with the garden hose, knowing she would thoroughly scrub it with hot, soapy water. She had a brown and gold earthenware crock that she placed all of her chopped vegetables in to salt down overnight with kosher salt. I would help her by going to the basement with Grandpa and crawling under the porch and carrying out the boxes of jars, all dusty and covered with cobwebs. Amazing how when you are young, spiders and icky bugs don't seem to bother you.

I would set the boxes on the back porch to let the icky bugs flee instead of taking them into her clean kitchen. The following morning she would have Grandpa bring them into the kitchen, where they would be thoroughly scrubbed before being boiled (sterilized) and set upside down on fluffy white dish towels to wait to be filled with the finished Chow-Chow. How I loved to eat the Chow-Chow with her delicious pinto beans, greens, and cornbread. Now that was some good eating.

Granny's grandmother raised her in Walhalla, South Carolina, after her mother died in a house fire when she was a child. She taught Granny how to make the chow-chow. Granny guarded that secret recipe. As much as I asked for it, she told me I wouldn't be able to make it like her and to just gather the vegetables and all for her to make it and leave the kitchen. She said the young folks didn't want to take the time to make it the right way. I remember watching her cutting piles of the crispy fresh cabbages and chopping green and red sweet bell peppers and mounds of onions fresh from the garden, along with green tomatoes. It made many a cold winter's night a whole lot warmer.

Unfortunately, Granny took that special recipe to her grave; she would never share it with anyone, preferring to make it herself. I have traveled to many county fairs and small-town farmer's markets, but rarely have I found a chow-chow relish that equals up to the goodness of hers. I have a couple recipes on hand that I am going to try; I am determined to recreate and share this family jewel.

Sugarcane

Grandpa was out back pulling weeds from the garden this particular warm summer afternoon. As usual I shadowed his every move, hoping I would one day grow big and tasty vegetables like he did. My mom was afraid of worms, so she rarely planted outdoors; besides, with three children at the time, her hands were pretty much full.

I went to the mulberry bush with my little bowl and filled it with the sweet, deep velvety purple tidbits. Grandpa took his hoe and chopped into the garden soil, aerating it and making the rich black Ohio soil receptive to the water and fertilizers he would feed it early in the morning before the full heat of the day.

He took his handkerchief out of his back pocket and mopped the sweat from his head. The straw hat he wore kept the sun off of his head and neck but did nothing to stop the sweat that dared to sting his eyes as he worked the earth. He walked over to the side of the house and brought back a strange green, purple, and yellow stick, which looked like the stalk that corn grew on with the leaves in it.

"Marthay, come 'ere baby," he said. He chewed tobacco and had just put a plug into his cheek.

"Okay, Grandpa," I answered, putting my pail down and running to him.

He took his knife out of his overall pocket and cut a small piece of the stick and held it out to me. I wondered why he was giving me some splintery shreds of the stick.

"Now you cain't swaller this, but jes chew it, chew it like gum..."

I placed the pieces in my mouth and started chewing slowly, and as I chewed a sweet liquid filled my mouth.

Wow, sweet stuff from a stick! I thought. *Only Grandpa could do this.*

"That's sugarcane, baby, now don't swaller it, there's more if you like it," he said, smiling at me as his warm, light-brown eyes crinkled.

Healing from Will's Garden

When I was twenty-six years old, I became afflicted with a mysterious ailment that rendered me incapable of digesting food. When I ate, it felt as if ground glass was passing through my digestive system. I suffered for months going from doctor to doctor. I spent several months in the hospital on several different occasions.

Whenever I was home from the hospital, Grandpa would be looking through books for vitamins and herbs to help me get well. I lost a great deal of weight and eventually temporarily lost the use of my legs. Doctors were baffled, but by trial and error they diagnosed me and treated me. Many of the medications they introduced me to made me sicker, or I was allergic to them. It was a very dark time in my life. I just wanted to be left alone, to die and escape the pain.

The weaker I got, the stronger Grandpa's determination was to figure out what was wrong with me. He would fix me bowls of oatmeal, bananas, toast, and vegetable soup from his garden and cups of sassafras tea. Most times it was the only thing I could keep down. He would pick up my weak body like a little rag doll and carry me to the car to take me to Dr. Hines, a man he trusted and believed could help me. Dr. Hines ran tests, took blood, and gave me B-12 shots. That gave me immediate but limited relief, but it was a start.

Grandpa was never too busy or too tired to care for me. He read innumerable journals, natural remedy magazines, and other books, looking for natural ways to alleviate my suffering. He would go to his garden and pick herbs and vegetables and prepare tonics and soups for me. Through my pain and tears, it seemed the love shown in his eyes, voice, and ministrations helped many of his concoctions to work.

Eventually the doctors discovered I had Crohn's disease, an incurable inflammatory bowel disease. Grandpa continued to read all he could find about it and found herbs, vitamins, and foods I could tolerate. Funny, the foods he had been preparing all along were the ones the doctors recommended. Grandpa was vital to my regaining my health and use of my legs and being able to once again function independently.

Georgia "Sugarcane"

While living in Georgia in the late '70s, I attended a family reunion with friends who had a small farm in Covington, Georgia. The reunion rekindled memories of times I shared with my grandpa. I spotted a stack of familiar-looking sticks on a wheelbarrow, and I pinched me a chunk of one of the sticks off and poked it into my mouth. My friend looked at me with a puzzled expression on her face. I tried to chew the "sugarcane," but it was hard, tough, dry, and not at all sweet.

Maybe they have taken all the sweetness out already, I thought as I looked for somewhere to dispose of the tough stringy mess in my mouth. I had been chewing a piece of the stalk that looked like the one Grandpa shared with me many years ago. My friend Shirley noticed my expression of distaste, and she laughed loudly. She said I was chewing on a piece of cornstalk.

"I thought maybe that was some kinda northern thing you were doing," she said. There was no way to hide my embarrassment, but it taught me to ask before I try something unfamiliar.

Years later in 1986, my husband, Calvin, and I took our children and left Cleveland, relocating in Georgia's warm sunshine, a few hours away from Florida's beaches. It was his first time living in the South and a return for me.

We loved the green spaces, the fresh air, the quaint farmer's markets and roadside stands where we purchased plump tomatoes, cool cucumbers, sunshine-yellow squash, and fresh corn on the cob. In the fall we enjoyed going to the stands to get apples, cider, and pumpkins that we decorated for Halloween and roasted the seeds to munch on. We did not miss the mounds of snow in the Midwest or the lake-effect snow that barreled across Lake Erie in the winter.

Broccoli

Each summer I would take my children back home to Cleveland to visit family, and we would always stay with my grandparents. Those were some of the most wonderful moments of my adult life. I would pamper them, cook special meals for them, and take my grandmother shopping to fill up her deep freezer for the winter. I would also purchase the vegetables that she needed for her chow-chow.

They were in their seventies, and Grandpa's garden consisted of a few tomato plants—Big Boys and Better Boys—a few cucumber plants, a couple green cabbage plants, and a couple rows of greens. Age had taken its toll on the both of them.

I made wonderful buttery pound cakes, peach and apple cobblers, and homemade ice cream for them. It was my time to just love on them as they had loved on me all of my life.

Of all of the veggies Grandpa loved (he had to have a baked sweet potato and slices of cucumbers and tomatoes fresh from his garden in vinegar *each day* for dinner), he had a strong dislike for broccoli, said it looked like trees and smelled bad, and he would never eat that stuff.

One Sunday I prepared dinner. I decided to make broccoli rice and cheese, but I did not tell him what it was. He ate two servings, and afterwards I told him what the casserole he enjoyed so much was made of. His jaw dropped, his eyes widened, he and shouted to my grandmother, who was sitting on the front porch, drinking her iced tea with fresh mint from the yard.

"Corine, Marthay done had me eat broccoli—and it was good! I like it!" Grandpa exclaimed, and I was elated.

I have even taught my children and grandchildren how to make the broccoli rice and cheese casserole at a young age, and they continue to enjoy it as well. This is a quick and easy recipe that is virtually foolproof. Today's "instant gratification" generation will enjoy its simplicity.

Martha's Quick And Tasty Broccoli And Cheese Casserole

Directions

01. Cook your favorite type of rice (mine is jasmine), enough for four servings. If you need a larger quantity, double the amount of broccoli that you cook.

02. Microwave or boil 1 package of frozen chopped broccoli, until done but not overcooked and limp.

03. Combine the drained hot rice, broccoli, 3 – 4 tbsp butter, 1 – ½ cup sharp cheese, ½ cup Colby cheese (reserving some of the sharp cheese for the topping), and 1 can cream of mushroom soup.

04. Add a little milk but don't make it too soupy, just creamy. Start with about ¼ cup and add more if needed.

05. Add salt and pepper to taste.

06. Pour into a lightly greased casserole dish, top with remaining shredded sharp cheese.

07. Bake in a 350 °F oven for about 25 minutes, until the cheese melts and bubbles. If you don't like mushrooms, omit the soup and add a little more milk and butter. Enjoy!

Grandpa's Legacy

One summer, not too long ago, when we went to Cleveland for our summer visit I noticed a big change. Grandpa had kept a garden for at least forty-five years, but this particular summer, he stopped planting his Big Boy and Better Boy tomatoes. He also stopped keeping his white plastic ducks filled with beautiful fresh flowers, instead sticking plastic replicas into the pot. He rarely even sat on the porch or listened to his beloved Cleveland Indians baseball games on his transistor radio, that relic of his, which was held together with an array of rubber bands because the battery case had broken off and they held them in place.

My Grandpa for many years religiously read and planted by *The Old Farmer's Almanac* and knew which herbs were good for which ailments. He voraciously read the *Puritans Pride* vitamin catalogs (he was probably one of their best mail order customers). Grandpa, who had long ago stopped chewing tobacco and smoking, was silently fighting prostate cancer, a battle he didn't win.

Today, every opportunity that I get to plant something I continue to do so, and just as he taught me how to coax the earth into yielding wonderful and nutritious delights, I have also taught my children and grandchildren. Alone with rich soil on my hands and sweat on my forehead, I can still hear his voice instructing me to keep planting and keep growing.

Will's House

Pla-ploop, pop, pop, bloop, bloop...

The coffee percolator sings.

Sssst, pop, pop, ssst

The bacon sizzles a hot reply.

Hot sticky cheese bubbles over the sides of the toast.

Buttery grits pop and boil.

Country music singers wailin' and bemoanin' love, life, and country livin'

Drift from the kitchen radio to upstairs rooms.

Grandpa taps the tips of his shiny black shoes.

I rush to get the homemade peach and strawberry preserves from the pantry,

And Grandpa's favorite coffee cup.

First I blow, then sip the spicy and fragrant sassafras tea

That Grandpa makes just for me.

Grandpa sleeps downstairs to protect his house

No one was "comin in heh" he'd say. "My family's gonna be safe heh."

In the South's cotton fields,

Beautiful, white blossoms transform, turning crimson,

Like the sharp cuts the bracts made on my grandfather's hands

When he pulled the fluffy white balls of cotton.

Sun high and hot, he wiped a drop of blood from his fingers

And drops of sweat from his brow.

"Crops gotta be picked."

Acrid smells of stifling Northern steel mills replaced those fields.

Steel splattered crimson, sharp edges, massive machines

Maiming,

mangling fingers.

Somehow I never missed them when I grasped his strong and gentle hands.

I run to his room and sit in his comfy chair

Noxzema, Spearmint, and Juicy Fruit, Old-Spice and Bengay live in the air,

Envelope me like the crocheted throw on the back of the chair.

I smear the silvery white Noxzema on my cheeks

And over my whole face.

I smell and look just like Grandpa; reflecting his warm caramel-colored eyes,

And smooth pecan tan cheeks.

His mammoth, circular mirror reflects his life:

Me, his Farmer's Almanac, worn Bible near his alarm clock.

His footlocker at the foot of his bed holds his perfectly lined shoes,

His shoe polish kit, and an old checkerboard.

I tear out of the back door, jumping down the steps

To help Grandpa in his garden. It isn't a chore, but a treat.

Grandpa is out back, making sure his transistor radio is loud enough

To hear "his" Cleveland Indians baseball game.

I step past perfectly round cabbages and collards tall and deep green

Into the backyard near the pear tree. I see Grandpa pulling spring onions and beets.

Long, cool cucumbers, okra, and plump, sweet tomatoes, nestled in his basket,

Where I place spearmint that I pulled for his sweet tea.

Quietly, expertly, coaxing the earth to yield to his touch,

He loosens dirt around the plant roots,

I sprinkle them with water from my tin pail.

Regal morning glories boldly scale up the side of the garage,

Spilling over the back fence into the neighbor's yard.

Marigolds jiggle their bright golden heads in between herbs:

Thyme, red clover, chives, garlic, and a bush of rosemary.

Wherever there is dirt Grandpa plants something good.

A patch of strawberries lines edge the thin path along the driveway,

And suddenly we are in the front yard.

Plastic ducks border the stairs up to the front porch,

Filled with scarlet geraniums, black-eyed Susans, and burgundy sun coleus.

Fragrant honeysuckle vines intertwine with fruit-heavy, sweet concord grape vines

I appear, from the cool shady side of the house,

Scratching around my mouth, embarrassed through the grape vines.

Grandpa laughs, seeing purple blotches of concord on my fingers and face.

The radio sputters and crackles the national anthem.

We put the tools in the garage and head for the large green porch swing.

The game has started; he looks off into the sky.

I suppose he is watching the game in his mind's eye.

C-r-a-c-k-k-k of a hit from an Indians bat, my arm around his neck,

His face crinkles into a loving smile.

He takes his white handkerchief and holds it under the water spigot

Wiping the sweet purple tint off my sun-bronzed face.

We sit on the swing and he pulls his pearl-handled pocket knife out

And very carefully cuts a piece of sugarcane and shares its sweetness with me.

Memorial Day

In the spring of 2014, I was attending Agnes Scott College. I looked into going on a cultural immersion trip to fulfill my foreign language requirements in a unique fashion. Memorial Day was filled with the anticipation of going to visit and study in Spain in just a few weeks. I had never been to Europe.

Instead of preparing barbecue, salads, and baked beans, I was getting set for my trip, and I began to think of re-memories of some of the holiday celebrations that I shared with my family throughout the years. Most were filled with happy memories, and others were memorable for other reasons. Like the time my mother went into labor during our cookout with my sister LaWanda, or the first time I experienced the pain of seeing a sibling injured in the midst of a holiday celebration.

After the harsh, cold Cleveland winters, my siblings and I looked forward to the springtime thaw. We craved the warm sun and family fun that summer brought in. My family enjoyed cookouts and threw one as soon as the weather permitted. American flags flew amidst the mouthwatering clouds of smoke from Daddy's grill on the summer holidays. There would be laughter, hugs, and wet kisses mashed on our faces. With such a large family, we always ran short of something, but my mother made sure we were never short of love. We would enjoy fruity "Little Tom sodas" and homemade, hand-cranked creamy vanilla ice cream.

Raising a family of seven children could sometimes be a challenge. On those days, any illness, unhappiness, fear, or lack would cease to exist. Except the Memorial Day when I was eleven years old.

Tony was the next oldest sibling to me, my younger brother. He had smooth Hershey chocolate skin, soft curly hair, and large round eyes that held pain and many mysteries we had yet to see. He had dimpled cheeks and long lashes that girls would love to have. I loved my Tone-Tone from the first day I laid eyes on him. When Mama brought him home from the hospital, his tiny fingers wrapped around my finger and my heart. He was four years younger than I was, quiet and kindhearted. Since I was an only child for four years, he was a warm, wonderful, tiny person I could love on anytime I wanted to. Even after the births of my other siblings, there was still a very special bond between us.

Memorial Day morning, we were all excited for our first big cookout for the year, and I was inside the house helping prepare food to be cooked. As the oldest daughter, along with helping look after my siblings, it was expected that I help Mama in the kitchen.

The old folks used to say, "She's a right smart girl, helping her mama and all."

It wasn't a choice; it was a silent expectation that could become a loud protestation if the girls did not help their mother around the house. Clearly we grew up with gender roles assigned as to what girls'/women's work was, and what boys'/men's roles were within a family. I had picked the navy beans for the baked beans the night before, snapped the fresh green beans from my grandpa's garden, peeled potatoes, and carefully chopped celery and onions for Mama's potato salad. Besides her buttery yeast rolls, her potato salad was a family favorite.

Mama's Potato Salad

Ingredients

- 6 potatoes boiled, peeled, and cut into bite-sized pieces

- 1 tbsp mustard

- 5 boiled eggs

- 3 – 4 tbsp Mayo or Miracle Whip (also a matter of taste)

- ¼ – ½ cup each of finely chopped celery and onions (based on your preference)

- 2 – 3 tbsp sweet pickle relish (or more to your taste)

- ½ tbsp cider vinegar

- Salt and pepper to taste

Directions

01. Combine all the ingredients.

02. Place two sliced boiled eggs on top and sprinkle paprika lightly.

03. Chill then enjoy.

Mama and Daddy washed and seasoned the chicken and slabs of ribs while waiting on the coals on the grill to get just right. Daddy had made his sweet, tangy, sticky barbecue sauce a couple of days earlier and had retrieved the lemon halves and bay leaves from it while it simmered, popping like buttery cheese grits on a cold morning.

My family shared the driveway on the house on 82nd and Quincy in Cleveland, Ohio, with an elderly couple who had fenced in most of their property and were not in the least bit sociable. In hindsight, the thought of seven or eight kids running around, with friends squealing, and Daddy's big trucks rumbling to the backyard probably did not endear us to them. In our part of the backyard, Daddy parked his dump truck and car. He had an assortment of metals, tools, and tires on one side and was recycling before we knew what it was.

Earlier in the spring, after the snow had melted, Daddy surprised us with a playground set in our own backyard. When it got warm we wouldn't have to walk down to the schoolyard to play. Imagine that—us kids had a swing set and sliding board in the very back part of our own yard where we could safely play. No one ever thought about cementing the playground equipment down, it was in an open and grassy area, and we were just glad to have use of it. While the grill was sizzling, the kids could play in back on the playground set.

Daddy's barbecue sauce was his own creation. First, he got a sturdy cast iron pot and poured a bottle of catsup into it. He never measured anything but it always came out right. He added a couple cans of tomato paste after that, rinsing each out twice, pouring the water from the cans into the pot each time. He poured a couple of glugs of cider vinegar (⅓ cup), some brown sugar (about ¾ cup), and if more was added he would adjust the whole recipe. He liked it sweet, spicy, slightly lemony, and with a couple squirts of regular yellow mustard in it, stirred over medium heat. Meanwhile one of us kids rolled two lemons on the tabletop (to help the juices flow freely when he cut them) and squeezed them into the sauce. After he squeezed in the juice, he quartered them and tossed them into the sauce. He chopped up an onion and some garlic next, and then he added a couple of bay leaves into the fragrant, gently bubbling pot. Occasionally I saw him empty half a can of beer into the sauce as well. The smell invaded our senses, causing an elevated sense of anticipation for the meat that was to be done soon.

My younger siblings had gathered to take turns turning the crank on the ice cream freezer and alternately added gravel to the Little Tom soda bottles that they were washing in a huge-warm-soapy-water-filled galvanized steel washtub. Shaking the gravel in the bottles would loosen any sticky stuff that was in the bottom. Once they were finished, Daddy would take them to Mr. Stanley's corner store and redeem the crystal clean empty bottles for sweet, fruity-filled orange, peach, grape, cherry, and strawberry soda pops. The washtub would turn into a massive ice bucket in the backyard filled with Little Toms. The kid-sized seven-ounce bottles of delight mingled with chilling Carling Black Label beer for the adults. Early mornings in our neighborhood were permeated by the yeasty aroma from the Carling brewery; we imagined that it was delicious hot bread we smelled instead of beer.

The burgers and hot dogs were also ready for the grill in between cooking the various meats. We knew that if we got our chores done, we could go play as the rest of the adults arrived and prepared their additions to the day's meal. Later, Granny would check on the ice cream and when it was time, add delicious fresh strawberries.

My grandmother, her twin sister Catherine, and my grandfather arrived around 1:00 p.m. with turnip greens, potato chips, popsicles, more beer, and a couple of cold watermelons in their arms. Granny also had a basket of plump, purple, sweet concord grapes from their vines along the side of her house.

Daddy had gone to the store earlier, and our Little Toms were sweating sweetly in ice. The meat sizzled and Daddy's radio blared from the back porch: Aretha, James Brown, and

Marvin Gaye belted out songs that made you snap your fingers and move your feet. Grandpa twirled Granny around and displayed some fancy footwork, Aunt Cathy shook her hips and snapped her fingers while my sisters and I laughed, watching and whirling our hula hoops to the music. Daddy slid his arms around Mama's waist after poking a sample of his tender barbecued ribs into her smiling mouth.

My brothers and their friends were in the back yard with some of their friends near the sliding board playing "Billy Goats Gruff." The fence in the next yard had glass storm doors leaning against. The game consisted of one of the kids climbing to the top of the slide while the other person (the troll) rocked the slide from side to side. When a child got to the top of the slide, the troll would rock it to warn them to get off of his bridge. As I travelled back and forth from the kitchen to the backyard, I caught glimpses of Tony and the other kids as they played the game.

From the kitchen where I was finishing up the vegetables, I heard a crashing of glass and metal. Someone was screaming in agony—Tony!

I ran to the back yard as fast as I could. Children ran past me screaming and yelling with fear pasted across their formerly jubilant faces. The sliding board was nearly on its side, and my little brother was looking dazed lying on the ground. My other siblings were shaking and crying looking for Mama and Daddy.

I crawled under the slide and tried to lift him, and Tony turned to me and the right side of his face was missing. Where there was once smooth brown skin was now white meat hanging by a thread of skin. A neat slice separated his outer layer skin from the pink and white layers of his inner cheek. Tears of shock spilled from his eyes and he looked into my terrified face and mirrored my expression. Neither of us said a word to each other, I just jumped and ran from him.

I screamed. Crying hysterically and yelling, "Tony's face is cut off! Help us somebody please!"

My aunt and parents pushed past me and quickly carried him to my dad's car. My grandparents tried to calm us all down as they finished cooking the food. All I could do was cry for my little brother; I had never seen anything like it. I felt so guilty that I could not prevent his accident or take away his pain. I wasn't the protector that I promised that I would be for him when he was born. My heart was torn, I loved my Tone-Tone and had never seen any of our family members injured or bleeding. I knew that when Tony was on there, it must have tipped too far. As it fell, his elbow hit one of the glass doors leaning on the back fence and the glass sliced his cheek, barely missing his ear. I didn't know what to do to help him. Except get our parents. I felt so sick inside. My stomach twisted and my eyes refused to stop the flow of tears. When it was dinnertime, I couldn't bear to eat anything, I had to know he was okay.

Later that evening my Tone-tone returned home with a heavily bandaged and sedated face. His beautiful brown eyes peered out of the massive gauze ball that covered his head and most of his face. He had nearly 100 stitches and eventually had to undergo surgery and grafts to repair his face.

I held him so very closely. Hovering and following his every step, I refused to let him out of my sight. I pulled my chair close to him as he sat at the dining room table, and he squirmed and peered at me through his heavily bandaged face. He just wanted to eat some of the barbecue. To my own shock, with tiny anesthetized bites he was able to enjoy his dinner. As he ate, I wiped away tears creeping from my eyes. I had no desire to share the tasty dishes that had been prepared. All I wanted to do was to be close and watch over him. I was so grateful that he was back at home and would be okay. For Tony, in spite of his accident, the meal offered comfort as well as sustenance. Sadly, I have no recollection of the taste of that highly anticipated holiday meal, or any other family celebrations that year.

Life Happens

Tony loved Delmonico steaks, smooth jazz, cold beer, and sharp clothes. Our childhood bonds grew stronger as we grew older; he would always be my Tone-Tone, my little brother. Tony always looked to me for answers and explanations about most anything, places, cooking, books, and life in general. I was my brother's go-to girl. Over the years he grew into a quiet, gentle, and loving man who was considered a deep thinker. Tony had an exotic look: silky, loosely curled black hair, large coffee brown eyes, and a nearly hairless face. While in Atlanta he was often asked whether he was middle eastern or from east Africa. Once we had flown to Silver Springs Maryland for a family reunion and he was detained by the TSA at the airport. Even when we were returning to Atlanta, based solely on his appearance and their biased perceptions, he was stopped. He stood nearly six feet tall, and was slim, with just a smooth, slightly raised zigzag on his cheek from that childhood accident. The old folks would say that he was "a tall, cool drink of water."

Most people really never noticed the scar from that fateful Memorial Day, years ago, but more so his gentle ways, warm eyes, and big heart. He was mellow and laid back. A knowledgeable person who loved reading, Tony captured your attention because he knew so many little known facts and kept up with trivia and current affairs.

His clothes always fit like they were specially made just for him. He had his own fashion sense, not opting to wear everything everyone else chose, but he selected pieces that were laid back, distinguished and soft spoken like him. Tony preferred soft, warm burgundy sweaters as well as neutral browns, pearly grays, elegant ivories, or calm blues. Neatly tailored slacks, with a slight pleat in front in colors that complemented his sweaters and a good quality leather or suede dress shoe would complete his look.

Tony, my two oldest sons and I originally moved to Atlanta from Cleveland in 1978 for a change of scenery. We were all snowed out. I was recovering from an extended illness, and Tony was between jobs. We had family in Georgia that had encouraged us to come down. We packed a snack bag—fruit, chips, sandwiches, chicken that Mama had fried, and juices.

We had shipped our clothes ahead of us to my aunt's house, which would be our temporary residence. We kissed our mother, hugged our siblings, and took the long Greyhound bus ride to the South.

No snow! It was refreshing; the cool spring mornings boasted brilliant blue skies intertwined with pillowy clouds. It was here that we learned the art of dressing in layers that could be shed as the morning chill was chased away by the Hotlanta sun. It was like we were on an endless vacation, a new place to learn about and new people to meet. The traffic had not evolved into the current gridlock monster that terrorizes daily commutes. It was not the traffic nightmarish destination of people from all over the country yet. People sat on porches and waved when you passed their houses, and smiled and said "Hey" in greeting. MARTA's Five Points station was an oblong plot of land where there were several benches and layovers for various bus routes. During that time, Atlanta moved at a slower pace than what we were accustomed to. We were optimistic about our new city and anxious to learn our way around it. Soon after we arrived, we began looking for work.

Tony had gotten a job as a prep person at Micks of the Peasant restaurant chain. The Micks menu included a bunch of chicken sandwich variations, fresh salads, and mouthwatering steaks, chops, and ribs. Tony generally enjoyed a meal there on the days that he worked, and usually selected a Delmonico steak. Was it a boneless cousin of the ribeye or a style of cooking that its name was derived from? I am not completely sure of the origin, but I am sure of the tender, succulent, satiating taste of that steak. Some would say that the name refers to a method of preparation from one of several cuts of beef (typically the rib cut) prepared Delmonico style, made by Delmonico's Restaurant in New York City during the mid-19th century. A Delmonico steak is tasty, thick, and well-marbled. Oh my goodness how they would sizzle in the pan when Tony cooked them. He knew how to do wonderful and delicious things with steaks.

As I said, his favorite was Delmonico, marinated and smothered with sautéed mushrooms and onions. He was the king of a mean steak. He had watched the chefs at the restaurant and mastered the cooking of the Delmonico. He started with a smile, some nice smooth jazz playing, and he worked his magic on those steaks. He danced around the kitchen—a dash of salt and pepper, the aroma of the fresh garlic filling the room as the heat released it. I remember the piles of onions and mushrooms sweating in butter on a low flame, waiting to slide around the tantalizing steak.

I would whip up a salad of fresh greens, spring onions, cucumber slices, and farm fresh tomatoes, not those chemical dusted, wet cardboard ones that are so readily available today. We would drink Erlanger beers from ice cold frosty mugs between licking the delectable juices from our fingers. They say "it ain't good till you get it on you." We got it on us.

Tony also enjoyed soul food: turnip and collard greens, fried green tomatoes, macaroni and cheese, pinto beans and cornbread. I would frequently make some and serve it with a shredded carrot salad with raisins in it like Mama used to make. We would also have a jar of Granny's chow-chow close by.

We spent many enjoyable hours together, and we were known to throw some amazing Saturday night parties at our apartment; I would cook and Tony would keep our guests dancing and partying. Some Saturday afternoons we would pack some fried chicken, potato salad, pickles, rolls, and chilled Erlanger's beer and head to Shoal Creek Park with our music and blanket and sit under a tree, people watch, and talk. When I started working nights at SunTrust Bank, he would take care of my sons and help them with their homework. Sometimes when they were trying to get away with some mischief they would look in Tony's direction and he would be looking right at them.

"Uncle Tony, take your eyes off of me," the boys would say.

Not a man of many words, he kept his eyes on them. He encouraged them to read and develop a love of books.

I remember one time Tony had on a soft grey cashmere sweater, soft purple and gray scarf draped around his neck GQ style, and grey slacks and slate grey loafers with tassels resting on top. He was sharp! He smelled good, wearing one of his favorite colognes, Lagerfeld. There was a jazz set and he and Uncle Wilbur were taking some lady friends out to enjoy it. Uncle Will drove them to the club. I was so glad to see Tony smiling again and interacting with people outside of work.

A few years later, Uncle Wilbur passed away. Tony once again became despondent. He often mentioned how he missed Uncle Wilbur and his siblings up north:

"Would be nice to ride up to Cleveland and see Winky, Vernon, and Karen," he would say softly.

"That's a great idea. You want me to check out bus or plane fares for you?" I would ask.

"Naw, I was just thinking..." he would say, with a solemn look in his eyes.

He never had an inclination to return to Cleveland after Mama died, even though our siblings urged him to come back home. Mentally he was deteriorating and had to eventually be treated for depression. After Uncle Wilbur's death, I saw the flatness return to Tony's eyes, and occasionally he seemed irritable and unusually terse. He kept talking about "level thirteen" and how books held knowledge and that knowledge was power. He began collecting books—old, torn, mildewed books—and insisting that people take the knowledge he was trying to give them.

Tony walked away with his books. He moved to Augusta and lived without contacting anyone in our family for two years. My youngest sister and I called various agencies trying to locate him, but with privacy laws in place, they only took our contact info and said they would pass it along, if they found him.

Eventually he called me; he was back in Atlanta at a facility for people having mental episodes. Finally my siblings were all able to reconnect. Tony was back in our lives.

In time, Tony was eventually able to live independently and have his own apartment and job. Every other week I would go by his apartment and take him shopping. His apartment was a ten-minute drive from my house. That evening we would enjoy movies and a meal I prepared just for him.

In March of 2007, we went on our usual shopping trip; he had gotten his income tax refund and wanted to buy some clothes and other items for his apartment. While shopping he picked out a cream-colored guayabera shirt that was clearly too small for him. I held it up to him and suggested that we get a larger size.

"No, I want this one!" he shouted, surprising me with his anger.

"Okay," I answered, still puzzled at this personality change. I looked into his eyes, but he turned his head the other way. Unusually irritable, he finished shopping and said that he wanted to go straight back to his place, foregoing our usual movie night and dinner. Said he was just tired, of his job, his apartment, of Georgia—he just needed some time alone to think.

That was the final time I saw my Tone-tone. A couple of days later Tony walked away from his apartment, his job, and his loved ones without a trace. His job called me saying that he had not been to work that week, nor had he called in. I went to his apartment, and management opened the door; he was not there and his purchases from the prior weekend were still in the bags. Clearly when Mama died, it left a huge void in all of our lives, but for Tony a part of him went with her.

Like Mama, Tony will always be a light in our hearts, and I believe that one day, I will cross my Tone-Tone's path again. I often think of the times that we enjoyed life together—I miss it, and I miss Tony. I miss his laughter and smile. I miss him cooking that Delmonico steak. Tony was the second of my mother's seven children. Even as we grew older, I continued to be protective of him; he will always be my Tone-Tone. I will continue to keep my eye out for him as I travel around the city, and continue to make inquiries to the authorities. I feel as if he is still very close, though far away. Each day as I move about the city, walking, on MARTA, or riding in a car, I glance all around hoping to one day see Tony.

Part II

Tastes Like Home Feels

Nostalgia

When we were growing up in Cleveland, after the lake effect snow, gray mushy slush, and shoveling of what seemed like never-ending snow, we all looked forward to the thaw, the renewal, and the warm sun that springtime would bring.

Easter Sunday finally arrived as we were looking brand new. With coily Shirley Temple curls bouncing and our new Easter outfits on, we knew that we were something special. My three sisters and I walked to church with our stiff, scratchy, new petticoats under lovely pastel, flowered or pleated dresses, and shiny white patent leather shoes. Easter bonnets were perched on our heads, tiny white gloves on our hands. We were careful not to crush our springy curls. Head held high, we strode swinging cute little purses as we walked to church (my ears bearing singes from the straightening comb or hot curlers at the beauty shop the day before. There is nothing comparable to the acrid smell of your own sizzling flesh.) Didn't matter now, I looked good—I had learned early on that you had to suffer for beauty.

With Tony leading the way, my brothers strolled along proudly in their starched and stiff shirts, fresh haircuts, and Easter suits with ties tight around their necks. They occasionally let their eyes scan the homes we passed to see who all saw them, all decked out in their Easter suits.

Like us girls, they were determined to remember all of the parts of our Easter speech recitations. Our family would be there to see us in our finery, and we just couldn't disappoint them. Besides, we knew the treats awaiting us at home. There was a big brown-sugar-and-clove glazed ham, decorated with pineapples and maraschino cherries held by toothpicks whose glazed tips had bronze in them. Simmering on the stove were the fresh green beans I had helped snap, while hot and cheesy macaroni and cheese bubbled in the oven. Mama's mouthwatering homemade yeast rolls and potato salad, with just enough vinegar and mustard to make you smack your lips and smile down at the thin slices of boiled eggs decorating them, completed the feast. Of course we were also waiting to raid our Easter baskets for the plethora of sweets inside.

When my children were young, I occasionally wanted to recreate memories and dishes from my childhood for them. Since a couple of my children were born after my parents had passed away, they missed out on the "Grandparenting love" that I had experienced with my grandparents and godparents. I often told them stories about my childhood and life as a child in a house with seven siblings. As I recalled some of our favorite dishes that my parents cooked, I decided to make some for our July 4h cookout.

My daddy ruled the barbecue grill. Mama would help him wash and season the meats, and then my sisters and I would help her prepare the side dishes. My brothers were outside helping Daddy wherever needed. Daddy put the sizzle and smacking of lips in his "Q." His sweet and spicy sauce was certain to drip down your chin, tease, then escape your tongue, and cause eye rolling of the "slap your mama" good variety. I was going to cook the meat with a replica of Daddy's sauce, Mama's potato salad, and made-from-scratch baked beans.

The night before the cookout, I got the dried navy beans, molasses, mustard, tomato paste, dark brown sugar, bacon, and a chopped onion. We gathered around the counter and they watched me pick and sort the beans to make sure there wasn't any dirt or rocks mixed in. Of the five of my children, the oldest two drifted away to the television during that process. They had experienced this with my parents and grandparents. I rinsed the beans, happily talking about how my mom and grandmother made them for a side dish whenever we had cookouts. I covered the beans with cold water and soaked them overnight. The following morning, in a large ovenproof casserole dish, I placed the rinsed and drained beans inside with cut-up pieces of bacon and the chopped onion that I had sautéed in the bacon grease. My children were excited that the beans had "magically gotten bigger and drank some of the water" that was in the bowl. I added the remainder of the ingredients and let my daughter stir them while her brothers looked on and tried to pinch pieces of the bacon before we put them in the dish. I put the lid on the dish and popped it into a medium oven (325 °F).

In a couple of hours they had the house smelling wonderful. The beans had to cook two to three hours, and it seemed as if every 20 to 30 minutes one of the boys yelled, "Mom are they ready yet? I'm so hungry." Finally, later that day, after all the meats were grilled, the potato salad was cooling inside the refrigerator, and the macaroni and cheese bubbled promises of good eating, the beans were done.

Proudly I placed my feast on the table and we began to eat. My husband happily sliced the sticky, saucy ribs while the kids gobbled hot dogs washed down with cherry Kool-Aid with freshly sliced lemons floating in the pitcher. I spooned the baked beans on their plates, cautioning them that they were very hot, so remember to blow on them. I smiled as I watched them tuck into the baked beans. One of my younger sons looked up with remnants of baked bean sauce on his face and said, "Mommee, these taste good, just like the ones out of the can." Needless to say that was the first, and last, time that I went through the process of making them from scratch. In the future I would save time, energy, and the heat from the oven and give them the ones "out of the can." So much for nostalgia.

Easier "Like Homemade" Baked Beans

Ingredients

- 2 cans (16 oz) navy beans
- 1 – 2 cloves garlic, minced
- 1 tbsp Worcestershire sauce
- ¼ cup dark brown sugar
- 1 tsp prepared yellow mustard

- 3 strips bacon, diced
- ½ medium sweet onion, diced
- ¼ cup molasses
- ¼ cup ketchup

For the Top of Baked Beans (optional)

- 2 slices bacon, halved
- 1 tsp brown sugar

Directions

01. Preheat oven to 325 °F.

02. Pour navy beans into medium stockpot.

03. In a medium skillet, add diced bacon, onion, and garlic. Cook until bacon is crisp and onion is tender. Remove from heat and add to navy beans.

04. Add Worcestershire sauce, molasses, brown sugar, ketchup, and yellow mustard. Stir to combine well. Pour into deep casserole dish that you can serve from.

05. Top with bacon and sprinkle top with brown sugar.

06. Place in oven and bake 45 minutes. Increase temperature to 425 °F for 10 minutes to crisp bacon.

07. Remove from oven and allow to rest about 5 minutes before serving.

08. The bacon can be omitted and ground turkey can be browned and added instead.

Winter Holidays 1983

I arrived at Mama's house on a cold pre-Thanksgiving Wednesday afternoon in 1983. It was sunny, but windy and cool. The autumn breeze caused me to tighten the soft burnt-orange scarf nestled around my neck. In spite of Mama not feeling well, she was determined to prepare the annual dinner. My siblings and I always helped her put on this wonderful feast. There wouldn't be much sleeping tonight; there were greens to pick and wash, candied yams to prepare, a ham and turkey to bake. The occasion wouldn't be complete without Mama making her crusty, buttery homemade yeast rolls.

As I stepped inside the door, my glasses steamed up immediately. Mama gave me a quick, one-armed hug.

"Hi Baby, I'm sure glad you got here so early. Got lots to do, working on my rolls, can't let no draft get in on 'em," she said and rushed back to the kitchen.

Mama took holidays seriously. She had Thanksgiving-themed curtains, tablecloths, and placemats, and pilgrim- and turkey-shaped candles all around the house. Each year, with my brothers' help, she displayed all of her grandchildren's turkey hands and pilgrims they made in school.

Several cakes and sweet potato pies sat cooling on racks, and my heart smiles at the sweet memories that scene evokes. The cinnamon-infused apple pies, bubbling over with goodness, hissed and sizzled, dripping sweetness in Mama's oven.

Grabbing an apron from a notch in the pantry, I rolled up my sleeves, washed my hands, and got busy. Mama was all over the place: checking, stirring, seasoning, and directing us like a great maestro directing and perfecting her masterpiece. I worked on the candied yams as Mama prepared her yeast rolls. My sisters washed greens and cut up potatoes for potato salad. R&B music filled the air; we worked and sang.

I looked over at Mama. Her shoulders drooped, and her ankles were thick and puffy.

"Mama, you need to get those ankles elevated, you been busy all day."

"Not yet, Martha, I gotta finish these rolls. I will sit down when I finish."

On Thursday morning, the smell of Maxwell House coffee teased my senses; it promised to be *"good to the last drop."* The turkey was roasting in the oven; the ham was done, with pineapple rings and cherries adorning it. The sweet potato pies had golden crusts and sweet shiny-orange fillings gently browned, and the carrot and chocolate cakes were frosted and displayed on Mama's cake plates.

"They almost look too pretty to cut," she said proudly.

Around noon, my grandparents arrived, Grandpa smelling like Noxzema and Old Spice mingled with spearmint gum. Granny's arms were full with her buttery pound cake, and Grandpa carried a pan of oyster cornbread dressing.

The cozy house gradually filled with our Thanksgiving guests. Some sipped eggnog, some, apple cider. My brothers pitched in wherever needed—straightening up, taking coats, getting more chairs, or just following Mama's instructions. The grandchildren played in the piles of leaves my brothers had raked together, waiting on dinnertime.

The aroma of the fresh collard greens from Mama's garden teased our appetites. The tables were laden with platters of ham and turkey, sweet potato pies with hints of cinnamon and nutmeg inside, buttery-hot yeast rolls, and an array of vegetables. We gathered together, and hand-in-hand we prayed. From the tiniest to the tallest, voices spoke of what we were thankful for on that special day.

A warm smile illuminated Mama's face. I pleaded with her to just sit down and enjoy our family meal. She ambled around asking,

"You need anything else? Hot sauce? Vinegar, another roll?"

After dinner we children began to put away leftovers. Mama had finally got off her feet at Granny's insistence and dozed off. Grandpa came into the kitchen and hugged me as he retrieved his and Granny's to-go plates.

"This dinner just gets better each year," he said, his brown eyes crinkling in a smile. "Y'all have outdone yourselves."

By Christmas Mama's health continued to deteriorate. Yet she was determined to have her normal family Christmas dinner and festivities. Every room in the house was filled with the decorations and spirit of Christmas. The fragrant and colorful tree held a collection of handmade ornaments and decor that we had made over the years.

As usual, Mama hosted a wonderful and memorable Christmas celebration despite her failing health. Concerned by Mama's swelling and breathing difficulties, I begged her to let me take her to the doctor. The day after Christmas was her birthday—she would be 49 years young.

"No, not now Martha, I am afraid... afraid I won't come back home this time." she whispered in a shaky voice. Her brilliant blue eyes tried to blink back tears.

I hugged her close, inhaling her essence, feeling her warmth that continues to embrace me after all of these years. I looked up into Tony's eyes as he was bringing some dishes into the kitchen. Though he heard what she said, he made no comment. He jiggled the dishes, almost dropping them, before gently setting them down. Then with downcast eyes, he quickly left the room.

Mama needed a heart transplant. A couple of months earlier, in fall 1983, her doctor had called all of the family together for a meeting. My siblings and I sat, listening attentively to words that would change our lives forever.

"Your mother has about a snowball's chance in hell of getting a new heart. The insurance company calls it experimental; besides, they consider a housewife as having a low value in the community," he explained.

"The values are based on what you contribute to overall society. A CEO of a corporation that provided goods or a service in the community is more likely to get a transplant than your mother, a housewife. I'm sorry."

Those ominous words disturbed us all. I could not believe that the doctor was actually being so blunt and emotionless—this was our Mama. After the shock of the doctors' words wore off, I was livid, and my siblings were angry and confused. We had been hearing about all of the research on heart disease being done and yet we were at the mercy of this nationwide insurance company as to whether my mother would get the treatment she desperately needed.

Most of my siblings were young enough to still live at home and were available to help her in multiple ways, but we could not heal her heart. Tony was quietly suffering the impending loss of the person who loved him first.

On March 30, 1984, after much media attention, public and hospital officials' urgings, and the intervention of U.S. state representative Mary Rose Oakar, Ohio's first woman to go to Congress, the insurance company finally approved for Mama to be sent to Pittsburgh Presbyterian Hospital for the care she required. She had to have a heart transplant in order to survive. It was also my grandmother's birthday, and it was the best present that she could have hoped for—her only daughter finally being approved to get the help she needed. Tony and our younger brother William went to Pittsburg and were her daily support system and connection to us in Ohio. I was unable to go as I had three children to care for, but I accompanied her to the heliport at the hospital and kissed her before they placed her on the helicopter.

Squeezing my hand, she looked hopefully into my eyes. "See, I told you I was going, I'm gonna get my new heart," she said before they were airborne. "Make sure that you see about your daddy

That year Easter came in early April, and Mama was still in Pittsburgh Presbyterian hospital; no donor had been found. I placed my kids in my birthday gift from my husband—a white 1984 Pontiac Trans Am with T-tops and a silver bird gleaming across the hood—and headed to Pittsburgh. This occurred prior to when the twenty-four-hour convenience stores and gas stations existed. I carefully monitored my gas and made sure my tank never got below half full. It was a cold and drizzly day, but I had a need to see my mother.

We finally found the hospital that afternoon. My brothers had visited during the earlier CICU hours. We were several hours ahead of the next scheduled visitors' hour, but I was determined to see my Mama. I just needed to hold her and kiss her sweet face. I found myself fussing with a nurse who didn't care that I had travelled so far or that I had hungry children and had to drive back to Ohio that night.

"No exceptions, Miss—come back at seven," she said through clenched teeth. As I looked past her, I saw a small, familiar hand waving to me. Mama! We darted around the nurse and ran to her. The children hugged her and she touched and kissed each one. There was not a dry eye among us. We were stunned; she had over seventeen IVs connected to her and was nestled tenderly on an air mattress and sheepskin to lessen bed sores. She was very weak but lively,

"You kids minding your mama and being good?" she asked "Martha, you checking on your daddy? How is Momma and Daddy doing?" she asked about my grandparents.

It was a bittersweet Easter Sunday as tears and love overflowed between my mother, my children and myself. Our last Easter together.

On April 26, 1984, the Thursday after Easter, four months after her 49th birthday, Mama lost her battle with congestive heart failure. My brothers were at her bedside.

After Mama's death, an emptiness settled in Tony's eyes that we could never fill. He was forever changed; he seemed to have lost the light inside that had made him who he was. Quiet and sad, his huge brown eyes held silent cries for help. In reflection, I feel so bad for not recognizing his turmoil. I just wanted to see about him, just as Mama would have done; cook for him, be his place of refuge.

In 1986, my husband, children, Tony, and I all moved to Georgia. It was the second time for Tony and me, and my husband's first time living in Georgia. Tony was reunited with a favorite uncle, Wilbur, one of my mother's half-brothers. They were kindred spirits who loved smooth jazz, nice sweaters and hats, a good chess game, tender Delmonico steaks, and plenty of ice cold beer. It seemed that Uncle Wilbur was able to reawaken the sparks in Tony's eyes and life.

They became virtually inseparable, and eventually they got an apartment together. Uncle Wilbur got Tony a full-time job at a company where he had been working for several years.

Today my siblings and their families continue to enjoy the memories Mama made. They often cook dishes on the holidays that she prepared for us, including the sweetly glazed hams, her potato salad, collard greens, crispy edged cornbread dressing, buttery sweet candied yams, and melt in your mouth yeast rolls. We decorate our homes with the decorations we handmade to continue her traditions.

I often imagine Mama smiling down at us and those dishes and decorations from the special holiday meals that she prepared.

Fresh

Fresh flowers, freshly showered, rain-fresh air, fresh vegetables and fruits, and freshly prepared foods—all are enjoyable to me. In our world of immediate gratification, we often forget that good things come to those who wait. We grab fast food, live fast lives, and seek fast solutions. We miss the enjoyment of picking a plump tomato off the vine, washing it off and biting into it, its sweet juicy goodness sliding down our throats, leaving traces on our chins. Or grabbing a firm green one, slicing it and seasoning it and in minutes watching it sizzle in its puddle of hot olive oil, dusted with a little flour or cornmeal.

Fried green tomatoes are so much more than a popular movie. I have a close cousin, Eric, who loved the way I prepared them. All I had to say was that I was about to fry tomatoes, and he would rush over to my house. Even after many years I still get requests from friends as far away as South Korea wanting to know if when they come back to Georgia, would I fry them some green tomatoes.

Early in life I learned about enjoying the fruits of the earth and my labor when helping my family in our garden. Nothing was sweeter or tastier than going in the backyard and retrieving the selection of the day: squash, cabbage, cucumbers, fresh spring onions, garlic, broccoli, and sometimes even sweet corn. Fresh picked was the very best.

We often had apple and pear trees in our yards, grape vines, mulberry bushes, and wild strawberries that we raced against the squirrels and birds to enjoy. Nowadays, you just don't see many of the fruit trees, grape vines, and vegetable gardens like there used to be. No one takes the time. Instead, they rush to the store or market—instant gratification, but not nearly as satisfying as home grown. There were many days that I gathered fresh vegetables and herbs to prepare, like crisp and curly kale, bold garlic, radiant red and golden peppers, and fragrant rosemary. After the harvest, ripe purple eggplant, yellow squash, sweet onions, and fresh zucchini were washed and spritzed with olive oil and laid upon the grill to roast. Delightful. I suppose I just love fresh.

The Tentmaker Job

A tentmaking job is defined as an activity of any person who, while dedicating him or her to the ministry, receives little or no pay but performs other jobs to provide support for themselves.

I carefully pulled into the strip mall, and we all peered around for beauty parlors or *barber shops*.

"Right there!"

My sons, Kevin, who was about thirteen, and Mario, eleven, looked back into my eyes as they walked toward the barber shop, questioning whether this was the right thing to do.

I smiled and said, "Don't be afraid, go for it guys."

Mario, with one hand holding the basket tightly, nervously ran his empty hand through his thick curly twists on the top of his head that bounced as he walked. Kevin was wearing his favorite red Ohio State jersey with his cap turned backward as he opened the door. They walked inside the building. Suddenly the barber shop door opened and Kevin let out a loud whoop. Jumping up and down, he ran back to the car. Mario followed closely, smiling and joyfully waving his profits.

"They want more, they want more," the boys shouted happily. Eyes flashed in delight and large toothy smiles covered their faces. The basket Mario grasped so tightly no longer held the carefully wrapped slices of pound cake inside; instead it was dangling loosely in his hand, empty.

Kevin raised both fists in the air, filled with dollar bills. He opened the back door of the car and refilled the empty basket with more cake slices—red velvet, lemon pound cake, 7 Up pound cake, as well as sour cream pound cake—and returned to the barber shop. Sun rays danced across the windshield of my green Mazda, causing Mario to squint and shield his eyes, yet clutch his basket close, careful not to spill its contents. In a matter of minutes we were approaching our next destination.

My sons were athletic and very competitive since they were very young. They played little league baseball from seven and nine years old. It was almost time for the new season to begin, and I didn't have the money they would need for dues or uniforms. I had been working a part-time job at ADT security in addition to my full-time bank job. ADT had moved out of town, and so did the extra money it paid me. I shared my concerns with the youth minister, Ms. Pam, at the Friday night IHOP (International House of Praise), a children's weekly event held at our church.

Minister Pam said, "Girl, what is your tentmaker job? What can you and the boys do together to make money?"

"We don't know anything about making tents..." I said. I was confused, what could tents have to do with my lack of finances?

"Let me explain. You bake right? Your boys can also bake; I have tasted some of their cupcakes, cookies, and brownies at our bake sales," Minister Pam said. "That's your tentmaker job. Instead of just donating those baked goods, sell them to make money for the things that you need."

I had never heard of a tentmaker job until Minister Pam mentioned it to me. She offered scriptural references about the tentmaker job. In the Bible, the book of Acts tells of Paul, who was a tentmaker by trade. When he traveled to spread the gospel, he supported himself by making tents for the various locales that he visited. Hence a tentmaker provides a needed service or product that has some monetary value in the community they reside in. A tentmaker at some point can be self-supported through their job or business at the living standards of the local community. A tentmaker may raise some donations for start-up or to supplement their income, but during their tenure in a country, they can, at a minimum, earn a living wage by local standards. Some may compare it with having a plan B.

On the way home, I discussed the possibility with the boys.

"People won't buy it, they will laugh at us," said Mario.

"They will think we are poor," Kevin said dejectedly.

Well, I certainly won't make Mother of the Year, I thought to myself. Couldn't keep my second job from leaving, couldn't come up with the extra money to pay for their baseball team dues, and now I couldn't make my kids feel secure.

"Well then, I suppose we'll just forget about baseball this season. I just cannot afford it," I said. The rest of the ride home was silent, except for the hum of indistinct songs on the radio.

The next morning, Kevin came out on the deck where I was enjoying a cup of coffee and an orange glazed cinnamon roll. I licked the warm glaze from between my fingers before it dropped on my blouse.

"Mom, I really want to play ball. Do you think it will work?" He scanned my face with sad eyes, looking for a sign of hope or affirmation.

"Well we won't know for sure until we try, son."

A hint of warm nutmeg and cinnamon in the air reminded me of the loaves of banana nut bread baking in the oven. I went back into the house, leaving Kevin to his thoughts. Just in time; the loaves were warm and fragrant with a nice sweet thin crust and an inside filled with bananas and walnuts. About five minutes later he came into the kitchen with Mario in tow.

"Mama what about that 7 Up pound cake you taught us to make?" Kevin asked. I had discovered the elegantly simple 7 Up pound cake when I was looking for an easy but delicious cake to take to picnics, potluck dinners, school functions, and church meetings. Not everyone was fond of iced cakes, and this was a perfect companion to a cup of tea or coffee. It was simple enough to teach my children to make as well:

7 Up Pound Cake

Ingredients

- 2 sticks butter
- ½ cup vegetable shortening
- 1 tsp vanilla extract
- 1 tsp lemon extract
- 5 large eggs (room temperature)
- 3 cups granulated sugar
- 3 cups all-purpose flour
- 8 ounces 7 Up soda pop

Directions

01. Cream the butter and vegetable shortening together in a large bowl. When it is blended add the 3 cups of sugar one at a time, beating well between the addition of each cup.

02. Add the vanilla extract and lemon extract to the mixture. Beat until the mixture is smooth and fluffy.

03. Add eggs, one at a time, beating well between each addition.

04. Incorporate the flour alternately with the 7 Up. Continue to mix well until totally blended.

05. Pour batter into a greased and floured Bundt pan and bake at 325 °F for 1 hour and 20 minutes.

06. Test for doneness by inserting a toothpick into cake. If it comes out clean the cake is done.

07. Remove from oven and after 10 minutes, turn cake out of the pan onto a cooling rack.

As a tasty variation, substitute almond flavoring for the lemon extract, and substitute Cherry 7 Up for the regular 7 Up. Add a couple drops of red food coloring and you have a Blushing 7 Up pound cake.

After the boys went to their rooms and talked it over, they came into my office, where I was looking over other cake recipes I had collected.

"Mama, you know how everyone likes your cakes. Can we do it?" Mario asked. "Can we try?" Mario asked.

Me and my tentmakers were about to tickle a few sweet tooths!

We took inventory of our baking supplies: butter, vegetable shortening, eggs, flour, sugar, baking powder, baking soda, confectioners' sugar, vanilla extract, lemon extract, almond extract (the real stuff), red food coloring for red velvet cakes, vinegar, buttermilk, unsweetened cocoa powder, coconut, brown sugar, and walnuts and pecans for brownies. Yes, we had enough to at least get started.

We pulled out the extra mixer. I had a huge, heavy, gray KitchenAid commercial mixer on the counter and a handheld one, and the boys were very familiar with their use. We gathered our array of cake pans: Bundt, square, glass, metal, heart-shaped, and loaf pans. Freshly washed and dried, ready for business.

Thursday, after the boys got home from school, they took the butter and eggs out of the refrigerator to let them get to room temperature. Kevin got out all the other ingredients for the 7 Up pound cake. Mario greased and floured the Bundt pans. Kevin unwrapped the two sticks of butter that had begun to get soft and plopped them in the large, gleaming, stainless-steel mixing bowl. Then, carefully measuring the shortening, he added it to the sugar, then the vanilla and lemon extracts, and started beating them with the powerful mixer.

Mario got his big sifting bowl out and measured and sifted flour. He took a spoonful of flour and flipped it in Kevin's direction, creating a small cloud in the middle of the kitchen. Kevin took an empty eggshell and propelled it at Mario's head; it missed him and landed at my feet. Mario rushed to me, planted a kiss on my cheek, and scooped up the eggshell and tossed it in the trash can. Sheepishly, Kevin looked at me, grinned, and continued adding ingredients to his batter until all of the ingredients were in the bowl. The motor on the mixer hummed like a hive of honey bees.

Meanwhile, Mario was on his end of the counter, measuring buttermilk for the red velvet batter he had begun to prepare, sifting flour and cocoa powder, double checking his recipe. The oven was preheated: 325 °F for the pound cake, 350 °F for the red velvet. The kitchen seems to glow with goodness.

In a couple hours the 7 Up pound cake with its golden brown crust cooled on a rack and the three beet-colored layers of the red velvet cake cooled close by. Their lemony-chocolate aromas hovered over the counter where they sat.

Standing back, observing my boys, I recalled their first attempts, remembering how they used to watch me bake, standing on tiptoes trying to see what was in the shiny bowl, hoping they could slip a finger into the emptied bowl and lick off the goodness of my creations. At times, it seemed they liked the batter better than the finished product.

Together we would create masterpieces. They were given the opportunity to bake cakes from scratch. We gathered all of the measuring utensils, ingredients, bowls, and pans on the long counter. We were going to make a carrot cake.

Ms. Martha's Carrot Cake

Ingredients

- 2 cups all-purpose flour
- 2 tsp baking powder
- 3 tsp ground cinnamon
- ¼ tsp allspice
- 1¼ cups oil
- 1 cup packed brown sugar
- 3 cups grated carrots
- 1 cup raisins (optional)

- 2 tsp baking soda
- ½ tsp salt
- ½ tsp nutmeg
- 4 eggs
- 1½ cup granulated white sugar
- 2 tsp vanilla
- 1 cup nuts (Pecans or Walnuts)

Cream Cheese Frosting

- 8 ounces cream cheese, softened (room temperature works best)
- 2 cups confectioners' sugar
- 1 tsp vanilla extract
- ½ cup butter, softened

Directions

I preheated the oven to 350 °F. The boys prepared two 9 inch pans by greasing them with vegetable shortening and dusting flour over it to keep the cakes from sticking. Kevin mixed together all the dry ingredients: flour, baking soda, baking powder, salt, cinnamon, and nutmeg. In a larger bowl, Mario whisked together eggs, oil, sugars, and vanilla for about a minute or so. In the meantime, I carefully grated the carrots. Grated knuckles are no fun and they don't make the cake taste any better. As a child I helped my mom grate carrots, and cabbage for slaw, so I had scraped my knuckles a few times. Both boys had also felt the sting of grated knuckles when they moved too fast or were distracted while grating something.

The boys combined the wet and dry ingredients in the larger bowl. Kevin stirred it together until it was smooth and then beat it manually for about two minutes to incorporate air into the batter. Mario added the grated carrots. I tossed the raisins and nuts in a little flour, just enough to coat lightly. It kept them from sinking to the bottom of the batter.

We poured the batter into the prepared cake pans and baked it for approximately thirty-five minutes. The smells of the warmed spices filled the room like a delectable cloud and caused involuntary salivation. We checked for doneness by sticking a toothpick in the middle; if it came out clean, the cake was done. Once done, I placed the layers on a rack to cool thoroughly. The boys took this time to put away all of the ingredients, wipe down the counters, and sweep up the floor. They also took the butter and cream cheese out of the refrigerator to begin softening for the frosting. As the cakes cooled, we prepared our frosting with the mixer and the boys fussed over licking the beaters.

Just watching my boys made me remember when I first taught them about baking; my boys had put on clean, fresh, white t-shirts to cook in, and I had on my favorite burgundy apron similar to ones that Mama and Granny used when they cooked. My daughter Mimi had helped me many times and was quite familiar with the routine. My young culinary students started out by learning the names of each item that was used for baking. Scruncha-scruncha—the scratchy sound from the sifter filled the room. I always taught my children, then later my grandchildren, how to bake from scratch when they were big enough to handle the sifter.

"What do you have, Mario?"

"It's a sifter!" He grinned while squeezing the handle continuously. At six years old he was a little vertically challenged, so he had to stand on a step stool.

"What do you have, Kevin?" I asked

"The whisk and I wanna lick it," he answered.

Kevin measured the oil, red food coloring, vanilla extract, and buttermilk, and poured the liquids into the shiny silver mixing bowl. A bowl of sugar and sifted flour sat close on the long, spotless white counter, near the apple-shaped ceramic canister set. Near the sink sat a bottle of antibacterial hand soap—we cook clean! I set aside my steaming cup of coffee and cracked the eggs into the bowl; I'm not fond of eggshell cakes. Mario added the sugar to Kevin's liquids and then sifted together the flour, baking soda, salt, and cocoa powder. Kevin stirred the batter until smooth. Mario added the vinegar and buttermilk and giggled as the mixture sizzled.

They poured the batter into the prepared pans. I had coated the shortening with cocoa powder rather than flour so the cake would not have the white flour showing when it was removed from the pans. I slid the pans into the oven. The aroma of the cocoa powder made the kitchen smell chocolaty.

As the cake baked, my daughter Myesha prepared cream cheese frosting with the mixer, and again the boys fussed over licking the beaters. Did I create cooking monsters? I wondered, smiling at them.

By Friday night the boy's cakes, brownies, and cookies were cooled, wrapped, and placed into lovely odd-shaped wicker baskets. They were ready for their maiden voyage. Would our tents stand or fall?

Red Velvet Cake

Ingredients

- 2½ cups all-purpose flour
- 1 tsp baking soda
- 1 tbsp cocoa powder
- 1 tsp vanilla extract
- 2 tbsp red food coloring (1 ounce)

- 1¾ cups sugar
- 1 tsp salt
- 1½ cups vegetable oil
- 2 large eggs, at room temperature
- 1 tsp white distilled vinegar

1 cup buttermilk, at room temperature

Directions

I preheated the oven to 350 °F. The boys lightly oiled and floured three 9 x 1½ inch round cake pans. In a large bowl, Mario began to sift together the flour, sugar, baking soda, salt, and cocoa powder. In another large bowl, Kevin handled the wet ingredients. He whisked together the oil, buttermilk, eggs, food coloring, vinegar, and vanilla. Instead of pulling out the huge KitchenAid mixer, we chose to use the handheld mixer. Mario bought his bowl of dry ingredients to the counter where Kevin was waiting with the mixer. Carefully they mixed the dry ingredients into the wet ingredients until just combined and a smooth batter was formed.

I divided the cake batter evenly among the prepared cake pans and then placed the pans in the oven evenly spaced apart. After about fifteen minutes, while the smell of the chocolate had us all about to drool, I rotated the pans (halfway through the cooking) to ensure they were cooking evenly. The boys turned on the oven light to check for doneness, looking to see whether the cake had started to pull away from the side of the pans. If so I inserted a toothpick into the center of the cake and when it came out clean (after 25 – 30 minutes) I removed the cakes from the oven and ran a knife around the edges to loosen them from the sides of the pans. One at a time, I gently inverted the cakes onto a plate and then re-inverted them onto a cooling rack, rounded-sides up. I let cool them completely. The guys had the pleasure of frosting them with cream cheese icing.

Each Thursday we began baking for the upcoming weekend. I continued to work my day job at the bank, and the boys continued their schoolwork, but on the weekend we were cake mavens. Our large country kitchen made it easy. The new black, computerized oven nestled inside of a brick chimney-looking structure permitted us to cook practically foolproof. With lots of counter space as well as the old-fashioned butcher block table, we also had adequate places to prepare and cool our cakes easily.

The kitchen sink was at the center of our counter space. Over the sink was a large window that provided a view of our large wooded backyard; tulip poplars provided lovely flowers on the branches that bluebirds, robins, and sparrows visited. Occasionally we would catch a glimpse of tiny hummingbirds, rapidly beating their wings and hovering near a feeder we had placed in the yard. Then we would return to our baking.

Mario learned how to make the best ginger snaps I have ever eaten, Myesha made the best brownies, and Kevin learned how to make the big twelve-inch chocolate chip cookies and decorate them. We have experienced our casualties as well; there was the time when we had several orders for cakes around Thanksgiving and stayed up late, baking... and somehow while waiting for the cakes to get done, we fell asleep and we were awakened hours later to a "caramelly" sweet smell. We ran into the kitchen and found black crusty cakes, looking as if they had been frosted with charcoal. It took several days for that sickly sweet smell to leave the house.

There was also a time when I was making red velvet cakes and the humidity just wasn't right and the cakes didn't rise. I ended up with red velvet cookies, and no more ingredients that night to make more. And then there was another time I was multitasking, cooking, baking, writing and I forgot to add the eggs to the cake.

We developed a group of regular customers. An art dealer in Stone Mountain ordered half of a lemon pound cake each week; he said that if he bought a whole one, he would eat it all. A well-known barbecue restaurant in Decatur ordered cakes weekly, and various barbershops and beauty salons in the Decatur/Stone Mountain area put in their orders weekly for their favorites.

We generally baked about four different pound cakes to sell in slices. Each cake would yield at least seventeen slices. We'd make one red velvet in slices, one triple chocolate cake in slices, and whatever special requests that we got. Yes, at times it was exhausting, but it was so rewarding, figuratively as well as literally. The boys got so good at cake baking that they were able to sell them to their friends who ordered them for special occasions. For birthdays and Valentine's Day, they made heart-shaped cakes and decorated them without my assistance. I even took a couple of Wilton cake decorating classes and taught them how to use the pastry bags to decorate their cakes.

Kevin began college in 2004, ending his baking career, opting not to attend Savannah State; their baseball team was on strike. Instead he was eagerly considering playing baseball at LaGrange College. Likewise in 2006, Mario also started to attend LaGrange College, foregoing opportunities to attend and play football for other colleges. He decided that he wanted to remain close to family.

Whenever I went down to the school for football games, I would prepare dishes to add to the tailgate feast, complete with cakes to share. Our family, friends, and other LaGrange parents always enjoyed our collaborative feasts.

The subprime mortgage industry collapsed while the boys were at college in 2008, and again, I was without a job. Kevin and Mario came home one weekend to sadly help move our belongings out of the house. No amount of cakes or cookies could save our home of fourteen years from the steel grasp of foreclosure. As we took our final boxes out to the truck that would take the remnants of our home to a storage facility, we stood in the kitchen, looking around it for the final time. I inhaled deeply, smelling a hint of vanilla, and lemon extract, and a whisper of cinnamon. A tear, laced with nostalgia, inched down my cheek as we closed the door for the final time.

Tents are portable; we would find another place to pitch ours.

Part III
The International Epicurean

A Taste of the Motherland: Excursion to Ghana

I peeked out of the window of the plane—the clouds were puffy and white, the sky a stunning azure. I walked up and down the narrow aisle of the plane; I was told that it was not good to sit too long; blood clots could form in my legs.

When I reached the rear a few other passengers were standing around, sipping on coffee, water, chilled fruit juice, or a Coke. Introductions were exchanged as well as the obvious "Where are you from? Where are you headed? Ohhh okay."

Soon I would walk upon the ground that my ancestors crossed, breathe the fresh air that filled their lungs, and taste the fruits of the land. I would stand in the golden sunlight, be cooled by the salty foaming waters, and tinged by their blood, in the Motherland. I could not recall a time when I had been so excited about going somewhere. With each tick of the clock the anticipation of setting foot in Ghana had built up like a huge balloon about to explode. My trip of a lifetime was finally occurring.

Our footsteps echoed on the metal stairs as we made our descent from the plane.

"I can't believe it," Christine, the student life coordinator, said as she squeezed my hand, tears pooling in her eyes. The full moon lighted our way and a comforting warm breeze wrapped around us. My heartbeat mimicked the rhythms of native drums that had been thumping in my head, a song of welcome. Tears squeezed through my eyelids. We reached the final step, looked at each other, sucked in a deep breath, exhaled, and together stepped onto the tarmac. Squealing with excitement, elation, and awe, embracing, we jumped up and down.

"Ms. Martha, we are here, finally here! We are in Ghana, in Africa. We have reached the Motherland," she said.

For me, at that moment, in that time and place, nothing else mattered. Not even the nearly nineteen-hour flight from Atlanta to Toronto, Canada, to Accra, Ghana. I had previously traveled to Jamaica, the Bahamas, the U.S. Virgin Islands, Puerto Rico, and various states in the United States, but I had never ventured this far from family and home.

Would I contract malaria? Have stomach issues from the food or water? Would it be unbearably hot? What do people in Ghana eat? How do they live? I had a multitude of questions and was very curious to find the answers.

Once we landed and retrieved our luggage, several young men appeared to carry it and guide us to our cab and hotel. I was astounded about how little I knew about Ghana. It was not the Africa that I had seen on television; emaciated, half-naked people running all over the place, men with loincloths and spears, and wild animals tearing through the savanna chasing our bus. I had recently seen programs about guinea worms in the disease-ridden water, so I was expecting to see sick, worm-ridden people standing sorrowfully around bodies of dirty water. It never happened. I saw cities, friendly people, automobiles, and an abundance of fresh fruits, vegetables, and freshly caught fish.

Nearly every African American that I know has referred to Africa as the Motherland. Africa, known as the birthplace of civilization, was a mystery and a wealth of experiences to discover. I know that my ancestors were descendants of West African slaves. When attending our family reunions, the elders told of Jasper Daniels, from whom my family descended. He was captured in an area near West Africa and enslaved in South Carolina, Daniels being the surname of his master. Ever since I discovered this, it made me inquisitive about Africa. For most of my life the chance of ever setting foot in Africa was merely an elusive aspiration.

That first night of our arrival, the darkness shrouded me like liquid midnight, dark, humid, with a sprinkling of celestial lights twinkling. I basked in the aura of being in Ghana. We were taken to the Coconut Grove Regency Hotel in Accra and met and assisted by smiling, courteous staff members.

The morning greeted me with brilliance and dry heat, almost the polar opposite of the nights. I got dressed, brushed my teeth, and ran my fingers through the curly gold that crowned my head. I joined my group for breakfast downstairs, where fresh sweet slices of pineapples, mango, and papaya sat next to covered containers of flaky, fruit-filled French pastries. Large silver pots of hot water sat next to packets of Nescafe coffee and tea bags. Mango juice, orange juice, and milk sat close to the bowl of sugar cubes.

A woman with a sing-song voice smiled and asked us how we would like our eggs. As we ate, our trip facilitator informed us of local customs and greetings. For example, I learned that it was an insult to hand someone something with or shake hands with your left hand. It had a double entendre—the left hand had other uses; some were not very hygienic.

After breakfast I grabbed my journal, cameras, sunglasses, and cash and headed to the bus. I applied essential fragrant oils to repel any insects I could encounter.

Fred, our driver, greeted us with a broad smile and began to give us an oral history of the city and sights we would see. I discovered that some areas in Ghana were not so different from small rural towns I had visited in southern Georgia and South Carolina, which made it vaguely familiar to me. Some people had makeshift shacks and stands displaying containers filled with an array of vegetables and fruits, such as whole and sliced ripe watermelon, small, incredibly sweet bananas, sweet yams, and stacks of cassava (similar to yams, starchy but white inside), larger than 24 inches in length and nearly a foot in circumference. It made me recall the roadside stands that my grandparents used to stop by whenever we took road trips through country towns. There were even live chickens in cages that they were selling and stacks of fresh and smoked fish. Children played close by, singing, chasing one another, drawing in the dirt with sticks. Babies were tied to their mothers' backs with brightly colored pieces of fabric as the mothers sold their goods.

Each day with two cameras, fully charged, my journal and pen, I charted my incredible journey. With my eyes wide open, I mentally absorbed every sight that I saw, to revisit over and over. On my third day we were traveling to Elmina and I saw many fishing boats and families along the road prepping fish to be smoked and sold. I can still close my eyes, quiet my mind, and be back on the beach in Elmina, listening to the Atlantic Ocean roar upon its approach, waves frothy, white, and foamy as they crashed against the rocks and shore, then softly retreating, coaxing millions of grains of sand to join them. I loved rising early to experience the sunrise in Elmina.

I saw an abundance of fruits growing wild—lemons, mangoes, as well as banana and plantain trees scattered around the countryside to be claimed by anyone, or no one. I thought about my childhood and the bountiful fruit trees and grapevines that were available. My grandparents had a cherry and apple tree in their backyard and plump, sweet, juicy concord grapes growing all around the sides of their house and up the sides of the fence and garage.

I had never seen a mango tree before. When we were traveling to Torgome for an African naming ceremony, we crossed the Kpong Dam on the Volta River. Just before our bus crossed the river, there were a bunch of trees filled with ripe mangoes. Several children were attempting to dislodge the sweet, juicy fruit. Each of the fruits hangs from a long stem of sorts. The golden ripe mangoes hanging from trees were reminiscent of a mother's swollen, milk-filled breasts.

A few days later, while visiting the W.E.B. Dubois Center, I saw my first cashew trees, brimming with nuts. The tree had a cashew apple hanging and the nut attached at the bottom. It looked like an upside-down red or golden bell pepper. The cashew apple is highly perishable but very healthy. It can be eaten fresh or juiced. Syrup, wine, brandy, gin, preserved fruit, pickles, and glazed fruit are also made from the cashew apple. Professor Okafur, who was accompanying us on the trip was from Nigeria, pointed the trees out to me and showed me the different parts of the fruit. He also provided previously unknown information about the cashew tree. He said that prior to processing they should not be consumed. He explained that the nuts had to be soaked in water and roasted to discharge the caustic shell oil and acrid fumes. Hand shelling of the nut was impossible if the shell oil had not been removed previously. The shell oil would cause blisters in the mouth and throat when eaten.

Fresh fruits were a part of each meal, and I enjoyed every bite. Pineapples with nearly white flesh were succulent, sweet, and juicy. Small but fully ripened bananas tasted as if they had been infused with honey. Watermelons, used to hydrate as well as delight the taste buds, were abundant, always juicy, sweet, and ripe.

While visiting Elmina we stayed at the Coconut Grove Beach resort. It was a welcoming entryway to the alluring shore of the Atlantic Ocean, only a few short feet away from the water's edge. I got up early each morning, before daybreak, and walked to the shore of the ocean. Unrestricted, I walked into the warm cerulean waters or perched upon a rock at the water's edge. I witnessed the fishing boats departing as the golden sun poked through the horizon. The sun peeked between the fronds of the majestic palm trees.

The loud, brash shrieks from the strutting peacocks pierced the dawn as villagers crossed paths along the beach, heading to neighboring villages to be among the first to display their goods for sale that day. Women balanced large containers of fruits and vegetables on their heads, some with children tied to their backs by beautiful colored cloths, striding purposefully in the early morning. Perched on a sun-burnished rock, wrapped in the picturesque African sunset, and cooled by the salty spray from the Atlantic Ocean, I watched the fishing boats return in the evening with their treasures from the sea.

Throughout Ghana, the variation in the land was staggering; there were large stretches of barren ground next to lush areas teeming with vegetation. In Accra I saw many similar looking trees, and I was told they were Neem trees. The Neem tree is fascinating. It is an interesting multipurpose plant that has various medicinal and an agricultural benefit to humans as well as animals. The Neem tree has antibacterial, antifungal, and anti-inflammatory uses. Neem oil also is a safe alternative to DEET as an insect repellent. It is almost a one-stop medicine shop.

The following morning we boarded a bus to head to Kumasi, the second largest city in Ghana. On the way we stopped at a village market where huge shea butter nuts were split open and the golden smoothness inside was for sale. Marie, the woman selling it, took her large machete and split open the nut like it was a watermelon. We gladly purchased the rich hydrating salve from her as well as black soap, a staple of many Africans. Stalls held large vats of beans, corn kernels, grains, rice, and smoked and dried fish for sale. Squealing, nearly naked children ran around, dashing in and out of the stalls. Goats sauntered by, munching on whatever they considered edible. The sultry wind carried the heavy stench from the drainage ditches that were close by, filled with trash, excrement, and rotting food. It made me very appreciative of our plumbing and waste management facilities back home.

On a more solemn note, on my sixth day, my emotions were stirred while walking through the Cape Coast Castle, then again while visiting Assin Manso, the site of "Donkor Nsuo," the former Slave River and market. At Cape Coast, with its infamous slave dungeons and the "Door of No Return," I could feel the oppressive shroud of slave trafficking and its horrors; it terrified me, and saddened me. It was incomprehensible to image thousands of human beings being packed into the small subterranean chambers, without ventilation.

Walking down into the dungeon, I slipped on the floor, coated with the thick, slick yet sticky remnants of human blood, excrement, sweat, death. The lime, sand, and time had not diminished the atrocities executed in that place. I didn't want to stay in there, but then I also didn't want to leave. It seemed as if everything was as it had been, yet nothing was as it had been. As I stood in the slave dungeons, and by the site of the last bath, there was heaviness, a sense of helplessness and sorrow enveloping me.

A few days later our group visited a couple of schools and a children's hospital. In the village of Atonka, a small boy walked up to me and slid his warm little hand into mine and announced very loudly and happily, "I'm gonna be your best friend!" while displaying a warm smile. The school had very limited resources; however the proud, smiling faces of the children overshadowed the lack. The masses of giggling children surrounded me, posing for pictures that I shared with them. I wanted to open my arms wide and hug them close, as if that would right wrongs, just like when my grandfather used to hold me; everything was right in the world in his embrace.

The buildings were made of mud bricks, and long, dried grasses provided the roof. There were no air conditioners, electric lights, or adequate current books or school supplies. The library housed old, sun-baked, antiquated books and a computer lab with not even one working computer. I found it difficult seeing children without the basic supplies and books available to receive an adequate education. It was uncomfortable for me. It was uncomfortable for our group, we really felt inadequate: we wanted to do more, help more, give more. The school supplies we had collected could not nearly provide all they were lacking.

We saw tables set up under a tree, where a couple of women were mixing large pots of rice and other indistinguishable foods. They shooed away goats that hung close by in hopes of getting some dropped morsels. We noticed that when classes were let out for lunch, only a few children went over to the women, who dropped a couple of large scoops of food into a dish for them to eat. Most of the children ran and played or sat in the shade. We were informed that only the children whose parents could pay for food would be fed; the others would not. It seemed so unfair.

We spoke with the headmistress and expressed our sadness at the children being denied a meal. We offered to purchase a couple huge bags of rice (upwards of fifty pounds) so that all of the children were fed. We were told that the women would accept the rice from us but would not share it with the non-paying children. How can a child think or learn when they are hungry?

Before we left the village, we saw a few people walking through it, selling a large amount of the little bananas with the big flavor. We pooled our money and purchased the bananas and distributed them to all of the children. They were ecstatic.

My journey to what I thought would reconnect me to the Motherland culminated after I participated in a traditional naming ceremony the day before returning home. We traveled to a remote Akan village and were greeted by the thunder of drums, elders dressed in tribal splendor, and families in traditional, colorful, ceremonial dress, dancing to commence the ceremony. Children strutted around in colorful garments doing traditional dances, and then women joined in. They came to our group and with gentle urging pulled us into the dance, the celebration. Prayers were prayed, traditional libations were poured, and I was presented a handmade blue and white bracelet and a clay pot with my Akan name on it: Ama Dzifa, which means I was born on a Saturday, and my heart is peaceful. I felt honored.

While the drummers beat their drums and the villagers danced with us, I noticed a cloud of dust coming in our direction. It was hot and very dry. Suddenly the cloud of dust encircled us, similar to being in the eye of a hurricane. It was clear and sunny in the middle, but the winds whirled around us, never entering into our circle, and eventually the whirlwind grew so tall we could not see over it. No one stopped singing and dancing, but the students in my group looked warily from one to the other. Then a soft sprinkle of cool water gently brushed over all of us. The wind ceased.

We presented our hosts (who told us that we were official members of their community) with gifts and tokens of appreciation. We boarded our bus and, as we were riding down the dusty dry road away from the village, huge raindrops fell. The sun was shining brilliantly as the winds whipped and rain poured down in a deluge. Everyone dashed for shelter.

The rain was symbolically the ancestors' tears of joy upon our return Later that evening we noticed small circular white orbs in the background of many of our pictures. Had the ancestors joined in our celebration?

Years later, I still reflect on my sojourn. Was there a re-connection to Africa for me? Not really—it was more of an intense, enlightening experience. I can acknowledge that my existence today was created by men and women in chains. My family is the progeny of slaves from this beautiful land. I am honored to have had the opportunity to step through the Door of No Return and walk on the earth, breathe the fresh air, that my ancestors may have experienced prior to the Diaspora. To feel gentle ocean breezes, taste the sweetness of the fruits: mango, melons, coconuts, the small rich and sweet bananas, pineapples and papaya, ripe and filled with sunkissed sweetness. Our dinners of the traditional dishes such as jollof rice, cassava, and grilled fish were unforgettable. The journey wove its kaleidoscope of history and cultures into the strong and varied quilt of my life experiences. The land, so very rich in history, resources, pride, and culture, permitted me to sample its sweetness.

In Ghana akwaaba means welcome. Each smile, handshake, meal, and cool breeze echoed this sentiment. I explored a land steeped in a history of turmoil, yet overflowing with welcoming people and natural resources. I am gratified that Mother Africa opened her heart and arms to travelers from distant shores. *Medasi* means *thank you*.

Jollof Rice

Ingredients

- ¼ cup oil

- 1 red or green bell pepper, chopped

- 2 onions, chopped

- 3 cups long-grain rice

- 2 cups tomatoes, chopped

- 1 cup green beans

- Salt and pepper to taste

- 5 cups water or stock

- 1½ pounds chicken, cut into pieces

- 3 – 4 cloves of garlic, minced

- ¼ cups tomato paste

- 2 carrots, peeled and chopped

- 1 cup cabbage, chopped

Directions

01. Heat the oil over medium-high flame in a large pot.

02. Working in batches, add the chicken and brown on all sides.

03. Remove the chicken to another large pot and add the water or stock.

04. Bring to a boil, reduce heat to low, and simmer for 20 minutes.

05. While the chicken simmers, pour all but 2 – 3 tablespoons of oil out of the first pot.

06. Heat the oil over medium flame, add the onions and peppers and sauté until the onions are wilted and translucent, 4 – 5 minutes.

07. Add the garlic and sauté for another 1 – 2 minutes.

08. Stir the rice into the onions and peppers and heat through for another 1 – 2 minutes.

09. Stir in the tomato paste to coat the rice and give it a reddish hue.

10. Add the chopped tomatoes and let them cook down for 2 – 3 minutes.

11. Pour the chicken and its simmering liquid into the rice pot and add the carrots, green beans, and cabbage.

12. Season well with salt and pepper.

13. Bring to a boil, reduce heat to low, cover tightly, and simmer for 20 minutes.

14. Remove from heat, let rest another 10 minutes.

15. Remove to a serving platter and serve with sliced hard-boiled eggs and a side salad.

Jollof Rice Variations

There are many variations of jollof rice. Feel free to improvise using whatever meats and vegetables you have on hand. Try beef, ham, shrimp, fish, goat, or pork. For vegetables, add peas, potatoes, eggplant, or mushrooms.

Beef Jollof Rice: Substitute cubed stewing beef for the chicken. After browning the beef, simmer in liquid for 45 minutes before adding to the sautéed rice mixture.

Vegetarian Jollof Rice: Simply eliminate the meat and stir hot water or vegetable stock into the sautéed rice mixture.

En Busca de la Paella Auténtica
(In Search of Authentic Paella)

"Mas?" my hostess asked as she pushed a small basket of crusty bread across the table to me.

"Mas pan?" she repeated, smiling. I declined. It was so very enticing, but I had to show some type of control.

My eyes scanned the table. A selection of *queso* made in Asturias. *Ensalada mixta*, a fresh salad that consisted of mixed greens, tomatoes, tender baby corn, with slivers of carrots, celery, and bean sprouts tossed and drizzled in olive oil and a pinch of *sol* added. A pan of sizzling sardines, the largest I had ever seen, separated us.

I had just finished eating my very first bowl of gazpacho. The coolness of the cucumber, richness of the tomato, and mellowness of the garlic, bell peppers, and Spanish onions excited my taste buds. I had a preconceived notion that I would NOT like cold soup because for me, the "s" in soup is for sizzling hot. Its goodness caught me totally off guard.

Ines, the lady I was staying with during my Spanish culture immersion experience, was an excellent cook and wanted me to enjoy the regional dishes that she expertly prepared. This lunch was definitely a winner! Each day, every meal was a new and exciting adventure for my taste buds. The queso was mild, rich, and a tasty complement to the pan, a baguette-like bread. It had a crispy outside and a dense, hearty texture on the inside, a perfect pairing for cream cheese, fresh cheeses, chorizo, butter, or oil. By the time I returned to the United States I was a convert; sliced bread seemed soft and stuck to the roof of my mouth (why didn't I notice that before?), while this (pan) bread could stand alone. I continue to long for the crunchy, soft deliciousness. I occasionally go from the bakery to the farmers' market, searching, sampling, trying to find an equivalent to the bread on Ines's table which she served with practically everything—including beans.

How does a tasty and hearty bowl of beans seasoned with pulpo whet your appetite? The delicately tender, disc-shaped pieces of some kind of white meat in the bowl of beans created an intriguing array of unfamiliar flavor. While the flavor was unfamiliar, it definitely wasn't bad at all. I looked up from my bowl to see Ines was thoroughly enjoying the dish. I tried to match her enthusiasm—I didn't want to appear to be rude or to be playing with my food. When I was close to finishing my beans, I subtly lifted a side of the disc and saw a tiny suction cup—octopus. I am glad that I tasted it prior to seeing the tentacles, because I probably would not have tried it and would have missed out on a tasty new dish.

Before the octopus adventure, I studied, along with my class, the history, food, and culture of Spain. My professor and his wife even invited us to their home prior to our trip in order to experience a sampling of foods that we would probably eat while in Spain. But I was still not prepared to have my epicurean world rocked by such delights. Visiting the various cities, monuments, museums, and artifacts was mentally stimulating, and the fine dishes my hostess prepared were just as stimulating to my taste buds.

Prior to coming to Spain I had so many questions and by the end of my trip, most were answered.

I wondered, would I understand the land and the people who lived there? Or would I stand looking confused and out of place? Would the smiles be warm as the bright sun that warmed me? Would the majesty of the monuments, museums, and cathedrals put me awe? Would the stars look brighter in Spain? How would the food taste?

As I prepared for the trip, I was both inquisitive and excited. I was reminded by excited friends and family members, "You have got to try the paella! There will be other good foods to enjoy, but don't forget the paella, and tell me all about it. Will you make some when you get back?"

"Of course I will, I'm going to get a recipe," I answered. I was determined to learn how to prepare some Spanish dishes as they are done in Spain, and paella was heading that list. Paella, the mystical dish filled with rice, seafood, chicken, and vegetables, was distinctly prepared. It was a dish I had enjoyed on various occasions; however each version was slightly different. I was going to Spain, and I would have an opportunity to taste the real deal, authentic Paella. Spanish food historian Lourdes March said that paella "symbolizes the union and heritage of two important cultures, Roman and Arab." Paella's popularity has spread past Spain's borders, crossing cultures. As other cultures make versions of paella, the tasty dish has been slightly adjusted based on tastes and regional preferences. Consequently, paella recipes went from being relatively simple to including a wide variety of seafood, meat, sausage, as well as different.

When we arrived in Oviedo, I was met at the train station by my "host sister," Ines. We were so close in age, she couldn't be considered to be my host mother. Ines spoke no English and was a friendly and knowledgeable lady. With my limited command of the Spanish language, this would be an interesting opportunity.

Our first meal together was several courses, which included a chicken noodle type soup, mixed salad, and bread with various cream cheese based spreads to accompany it. We also had oven-fried fish, drizzled in olive oil, and a selection of fresh and ripe fruits. There was a seemingly bottomless fruit bowl with green plums, peaches, apples, pears, *melones*, *paraguayos*, nectarines, and luscious melons. Plump, deep red cherries were always available as well.

Ines smiled across the table and started speaking very fast, in Spanish; I had no idea what she was saying, and I think my face reflected that. She abruptly stopped talking, and we dropped our eyes into our food then looked back up and burst out laughing—talk about an icebreaker. We both gathered our Spanish/English dictionaries and broke our language barrier down by the following week.

She and her sister Ana took me to the beach in Gijon that following Sunday afternoon, and we visited the monuments, churches, and area shops. We ended our outing by stopping at a cafe and eating hot crispy churros that we dipped in chocolate. A real local treat.

On a lovely and warm sunny day in Oviedo, I sat at a park near *"el comodo apartmento"* on a bench in a cozy corner with a beautiful panoramic view of the mountainside. On my right below the sheer white clouds, on Mount Naranco, El Cristo with arms wide seemed to keep a vigilant watch over Oviedo. This monument, the Sacred Heart of Jesus, was a huge sculpture in which the figure of Jesus is reflected symbolically embracing and protecting the city of Oviedo. It was a comforting sight for me. The warm breeze brushed my skin gently, and instead of burying my mind in the food memoir I was reading, I decided to people watch for a while.

Everyone in Oviedo seemed to be very laid back: family and friend time is important, as it should be. I discovered that Spain was an interesting potpourri of history, religion, fashion, food, architecture, and culture. Oviedo was a pedestrian-friendly city with lots of hills, neighborhood markets, fountains, parks, and ancient *iglesias*—Roman Catholic churches—some dating as far back as the year 848. To walk into historic structures dating that far back sent chills of excitement down my spine.

During my many independent self-directed tours, I saw people who loved good food, were very family oriented, and loved their precious pets. I saw many different breeds of pampered pooches dressed in soccer jerseys, t-shirts, and other doggy-styled outfits. It was pleasurable watching the dogs bring out the inner-child of their owners, having them walk, run with them, tossing balls and other fetch toys or just rolling around in the grass, rubbing and wrestling with them. Praise and treats for the pets were plentiful, and regardless of breed, big or small, they were the most well-behaved dogs I had ever encountered. Just walking by one of the numerous outdoor cafes, as their owners nibbled on pequeno bocadillos, sipped on their bebida favorita, or chatted with friends and family, the canine companions patiently sat close by for what could have been hours, people watching.

My journey commenced and culminated in Madrid. The morning of my arrival, I wound my way through the maze of the Madrid Barajas Airport, the busiest airport in Spain. One of my classmates was also on the flight, so we shared a taxi to the hotel. It was the NH hotel, a Spanish-based hotel chain headquartered in Madrid. It was clean, comfortable, and close to shopping, restaurants, and transportation. I had a full street view of traffic, people, and places to eat close by. Once settled in my room, I flung open the windows and deeply inhaled the air. Viva Espana. So much to see, learn, and taste.

We joined our profesor for dinner that evening. La Taberna Toscana was the restaurant where we enjoyed our first autentica cena espanola. The vegetables we dined on were fresh and ripe, along with the regional cheeses, Spanish olives, and crusty bread that also graced our table. The ensalada mixta had slices of tomatoes on lettuce, topped with tuna fish and drizzled with olive oil and sol. I didn't think I would like the tuna without the sweet relish, eggs, salad dressing, and chopped onions that I have been used to eating, but it was tasty. I now prepare my salads in the same manner, with the Mediterranean flavor—using only an olive oil drizzle, a little bit of sea salt, and a few drops of freshly squeezed lemon juice. Lip-smacking goodness, and a healthier alternative.

We also had a sumptuous lunch that week at the Asador Chiky restaurant, where I had the best sangria I had ever wrapped my lips around. During our days in Madrid, we experienced many wonderful eateries, and the authentic Spanish dishes that were served satiated us.

Madrid seemed like another Manhattan in its own right. While looking for a place to enjoy my first lunch in the city, I ventured into *El Cortez de Ingles,* which seemed to be a one-stop-shopping spot. The ground floor had a supermarket, hot food counters, coffee shops (yes, Starbucks is there), and other eateries. The higher levels of the store were reminiscent of Macy's or Dillard's back home.

I discovered a crowded little eatery and, along with my roommate Emily, had my first lunch in Spain which didn't seem so "Spanish"—it consisted of fried *patatas*, fried chicken, and a Coke. After eating lunch at the café, I decided to take advantage of my comfy shoes and my natural inquisitiveness and walk around the city to fully enjoy its magnificence. There were lots of monuments and beautiful fountains, and every few blocks there were tables awaiting your arrival, for café, tapas, cerveza, or cool and refreshing agua. But beware, someone may be watching you as you are watching the city in motion.

A couple of days after my arrival, I was on the Metro, heading back to my hotel, and because I was obviously a *tourista* I became the target of a *carterista*. He had a heavy jacket draped over his arm, on a hot day, trying to conceal his criminal intent. What he didn't know was that I am very aware of my surroundings. I had no problem grabbing his hand, bending his fingers painfully back, and shoving him across the train. Not bad for a *tourista*. Embarrassed and shocked, he cowered near the doors, and as soon as the doors opened he scampered from the train. Other passengers applauded my courage and gave thumbs up and "good looking out" signs.

Prior to leaving Madrid and heading to Oviedo, we spent a day in the Spanish city of Toledo, known as the "City of the three cultures." The city is truly on a hillside, a virtual fortress. Toledo was a multicultural and multi-religious city, an architectural masterwork, home to the Christians, Jews, and Muslims who collaboratively built it. It was pretty much a pedestrian area in spite of all of the steep hills and very narrow and curving *calles*. The streets had various-sized stones in them, and if you weren't careful you could trip. I didn't trip, but I got a fat, red, hot, swollen, painful blood blister behind my big toe on my left foot. It took a few days to heal but when I say my foot was on fire... Even though I wore comfortable, well-fitting walking shoes, I suppose that my feet were not accustomed to the lengthy walking excursions or the varied types of cobblestone streets. Despite my discomfort I was eager to visit other areas of the city.

We passed by the Convent of St. Clement. One of the orders of nuns from there was purported to have invented marzipan. The delicious sweets are sold in many shops throughout the city as well as at the convent. Their recipes, which they have preserved over the ages, date back to the times of the Romans and Moors. Following one of the famines during the sixteenth century, they created dough with the only products they had in their food store: almonds and sugar. Marzipan is the paste, cooked or raw, obtained from the mixture of raw peeled almonds and sugar. I stopped inside a shop that sold it and bought a couple of pieces; I wanted to compare the taste with what I had tasted back home. I popped a piece in my mouth and it immediately showered my mouth with a flavor and sweetness so fresh and delicious, there was no comparison.

My most notable highlight of that excursion: Toledo Cathedral, massive and absolutely breathtaking. To actually have had the opportunity to walk into the immense and magnificent cathedral is mind blowing to me.

When I visited the fabulous Prado museum, the Reina Sofia Museum in Madrid, and the Royal Palace in Madrid, I thought that it couldn't get much better. But each day, each excursion, seemed to prove me wrong. Each sight that I saw, each meal that I enjoyed enhanced the experience of being in Spain.

The following Saturday morning we boarded a train and headed to our next destination, Oviedo. We arrived on Saturday evening, but after breakfast on Sunday morning it was time to see the city. It was market time and the city was crowded with locals and tourists who shopped, ate, drank, shopped, conversed, browsed, and shopped.

During the week, I only had to concentrate on my studies at the University of Oviedo—Inez made sure of that. My meals and laundry were handled with care. Even on our final evening together, she would not allow me to help her cook. However, she asked a younger student who was invited to dinner that evening to come into the kitchen and slice up some tomatoes and help set the table. Perhaps that is a cultural thing; the younger persons assist in meals for older persons. I don't really know. But I do know that each meal Inez prepared was a culinary delight.

She introduced me to a regional favorite: *fabada*, a rich Spanish bean stew made of white beans and a variety of sausages, including the spicy Spanish chorizo, blood sausage, and a piece of pork shoulder. It was hearty and delicious, but I didn't eat the blood sausage. A bit vampirish for me.

We munched on chorizos, with crackers and queso, as well as clams tossed with pasta, lentils with slivers of celery and carrots, and delectable seafood paella. It had the largest shrimp that I had eaten and smaller shrimp, mussels, and clams in their shiny shells resting on yellow rice. I had developed a sense of trust in her choices of meals and was rarely disappointed. I had never had fresh, pan-seared sardines, pulpa, or small sweet crabs and shrimp that were so fresh that only a short time ago they had been climbing over each other on the ice that chilled them.

Masterfully she introduced me and guided me to Asturias through its foods. Most noticeable for me was the large variety of fresh foods available in the markets. Whether they were the plentiful neighborhood markets or the massive Super Mercados, they had a wide selection of fresh, unblemished vegetables and fruits. There were workers in the produce department that wore gloves and delicately handled the food. Customers were not encouraged to touch it, just let the attendant know what they wanted and with gloved hands they would bag up the requested items. This was quite a difference from the shopping experience at home, where anyone could pick up, squeeze, smell, and handle the fresh produce. There were meat markets that skillfully displayed their offerings each day in pristine meat cases highly visible to passersby. The meats looked fresh, clean, and ready to be prepared. The seafood was so fresh that it was not unusual to see large shrimp climbing over the ice and each other, crabs clambering to get over each other, gleaming fresh octopi and squid on display, and even fish, swimming in tanks, that you could select for your meal. It's no wonder that Ines never went shopping to bring back a huge number of bags of groceries. She could run downstairs and, depending on her preference for that day, go to the store of her choice and get exactly the amount of whatever produce, meat, or seafood she wanted. On many occasions I saw men stop by the chocolateria and pick up fresh pan on their way home.

On a sunny afternoon after classes, I went home and had a wonderful surprise. Ines had the table set for lunch: the usual basket of bread, the plate of locally made cheeses, the bowl of ensalada mixta, and... seafood paella! I found out that Ines could make delicious paella. I was so fortunate to be with her.

She set the sumptuous dish on the table with a slight smile. There was flavorful plump yellow rice that cushioned shiny shelled plump mussels, large succulent whole shrimp, clams, and tiny baby shrimp. I had never eaten mussels before or clams out of a shell. They were plump and tasty, and I enjoyed each bite. Seeing my delight, Ines smiled proudly.

Ines taught me the joys of other local delicacies, and I taught her "easy." Ines would busily run place to place to create wonderful dishes for our meals. Each morning she would be up early preparing breakfast and coffee for me. I assured her that she could relax, I could prepare it, and she seemed happy to be able to sleep in. I had never eaten mussels before and they were plump and tasty, or even eaten clams out of a shell. I explained that she worked so very hard and that simple, easy meals were also appreciated. I didn't want her to burn out with cooking for me. Once she understood "easy," she relaxed and continued to make wonderful dishes. Sometimes something as elegantly simple as gazpacho, or other chilled soups with a selection of cheeses, jamon, crackers, or tasty pequeno bocadillos and a glass of sangria was our meal. Coincidentally, we were both diabetic and kept a good handle on our glucose levels by such healthy eating.

I seemed to have never gotten enough of the cool fresh water. I drank plenty of water and enjoyed the strong *cafe con leche* that was readily available everywhere, without the Starbucks price tag. Sometimes I treated myself to the *cafe con leche* with Baileys Irish coffee on the rocks while I utilized the free wifi (pronounced wefee) at the chocolateria on the next block.

On July fourth, the University of Oviedo arranged a special culinary and cultural treat for us. La Espicha. They transported us all to Tierra Astur Siderríes, a huge restaurant the locals frequented. One side was open, filled with tables of foods available to eat and drink as you walked around mingling with other students. On the other side were placed big old cider barrels, where you could sit inside and eat. Our hosts from the university, professors, and students who had come from different countries and schools mingled and ate together in the festive atmosphere.

Huge sides of meat hung in the kitchen area and lay on a counter in front of it. The aroma from the sizzling meats was torture; so much goodness to smell. My first *Espicha*. Traditionally when attending *Las Espichas,* there are no seats; participants browse through that maze of tables laden with foods and drinks. We enjoyed a variety of dishes which included cheeses, meats, fish, breads, olives, and desserts that were regional favorites, truly a taste of Asturias. The menu included:

- Embutíos Astures (sausages Asture)
- Tables de quesos artesanales asturianos (local cheese selection)
- Hüevos duros (hard boiled eggs)
- Tortielles de patata (traditional tortilla)
- Chorizos na sidra (chorizos cooked in sidra)
- Calamares fritos (fried calamari)

There were also musicians and dancers dressed in authentic clothing who provided music and merriment. Even some of the students joined them on stage to learn some of the dances. Drums rat-ta-tat-ted, guitars were strummed, and bagpipes squealed.

There were huge barrels that were not being used for dining that were filled with sidra, a locally produced fizzy cider. Sidra of this region is well known as the best in Europe. Friends often meet in the afternoon or evenings to have a glass of cider with friends instead of drinking a cup of coffee. The added treat is to see how the Sidra is poured—in Asturias, this is a crucial part of the experience. The customary method, known as *escanciar*, involves pouring the cider from high above one's head and allowing the free-flowing stream to plunge into the glass. When you pour the cider normally, it ends up flat, but it effervesces when you pour from a height. It was a little tart for me; I preferred the sangria. It was a different yet unique way to enjoy the Fourth of July in another country.

The university also scheduled excursions to places that would add to our cultural immersion in Oviedo. Most memorably we scaled by bus the precipitous *Picos De* Europa. We reached a point where the buses could no longer ascend and so we got off of them and continued our excursion on foot. Breathtaking! I stood higher in those majestic mountains than I had stood any place on earth. "I am so high in the air that I feel as if I could just reach up and touch God's toenail!" I told another student. I was in total awe of the magnitude of the mountains and the beauty of the surrounding valleys.

Ines had packed me a sumptuous lunch, even though I assured her that I could do it myself. My meal had the ever-loved package of Spanish olives, an assortment of *bocadillos*, a selection de frutas de verano—plump sweet burgundy cherries, ripe, sweet paraguayos, and nectarines. Propped up on a large rock close to a clear and tranquil lake, I took in the view as I ate. Occasionally some cows trotted down the side of the mountain and walked to the water's edge for a refreshing drink. They had no apprehensions about walking among us. The food seemed to taste even fresher, better. I wondered if it was the altitude or my state of awe and relaxation that contributed to that feeling.

The week prior to my returning home, Ines shared some recipes with me, and we even went to El Cortes Ingles and got a cookbook (written in Spanish) that I am able to understand. My instructor Vanessa at the university also gave me the recipe for a Spanish tortilla—or, as her children like to call it, a Spanish pizza.

Professor Vanessa's Easy Spanish Tortilla

Ingredients

- 3 potatoes
- 5 ounces of olive oil
- 1 onion
- 6 eggs

Directions

01. Peel and cut the potatoes into medium slices and chop the onion.

02. Heat the olive oil in a large frying pan.

03. Add the potatoes and onion and stew gently, partially covered, stirring occasionally until the potatoes are softened. (At this point, after I remove the potatoes and onions, I toss some mushrooms into the oil and cook for about 4 – 5 minutes).

04. Strain the potatoes and onions through a colander into a large bowl (set the strained oil aside).

05. Beat the eggs, adding salt and pepper to taste; set aside.

06. Pour some of the strained olive oil into a smaller skillet. Place vegetables and the beaten egg into the small skillet and cook at a medium heat, using the spatula to form a cushion shape.

07. When eggs are set, flip onto a plate, then add a little more oil to pan and slide the tortilla back into the pan for the other side to cook.

08. Invert twice more, cooking the tortilla briefly each time and pressing the edges to keep the cushion shape.

09. Slide onto a plate and cool for 10 minutes before serving. Slice and enjoy.

The night before we left Oviedo, Ines invited another student in my group and her host mom to share a sumptuous feast that she prepared for us. It would be our final tastes of the delectable regional breads, cheeses, *jamon*, mussels, salads, olives, and other foods that were a big part of the Asturian culture. I would have to rely on memories of the fruity sangria and the delectable foods that had teased and tantalized my tongue.

Lying in my bed that final night at Ines's house, I reflected on my trip. I thought about all that I had seen and tasted. It seemed to me that Oviedo represented a mixture of what most of Spain is: old and new, modern and traditional.

Our group returned to Madrid the Saturday before we were due to return home. On Sunday morning we experienced El Rastro, Madrid's largest open-air flea market. It is said to be the largest flea market in Europe, with up to 3,500 different stalls, and it extended through several streets. We walked through an endless maze of stalls that sold numerous items, including clothes, jewelry, purses, shoes, and souvenirs. In close proximity were many bars that had cold beer and *tapas* for sale. It was a constant crush of people and it was in your best interest to be vigilant; shoppers were easy prey for pickpockets. We sifted through the crush of people to get last-minute souvenirs and reminders of Spain.

That evening, our gracious professor took us for a wonderful final dinner at *La Paella Resturante*. I had gotten used to the family-style dinners that we shared—face-to-face mealtime without the interruptions of technology, like many years ago when I was a child. It was a wonderful meal: the large hot rolls, the salad, the multiple conversations. Everything was delightful.

We excitedly shared the highlights of our time in Spain as well as which foods were most enjoyable—the breads, cheeses, fresh foods. Additionally, meals prepared by our host families and the meals that were coordinated by our professor were unanimously given high accolades. The huge pans of hot paella were delivered to each of our tables with much pomp and circumstance, sizzling and emanating delightful aromas. The paella contained seafood, chicken, and chorizo sausage, which was mixed into the rice and seasonings. We dug into our feast. It was good, but I must say that the homemade seafood paella that Ines prepared for me in Oviedo was preferable for my tastes. I had wonderful memories of the plump mussels, large succulent whole shrimp, clams, and tiny baby shrimp tucked in the yellow rice that she had used. Mi búsqueda habia teminada. La paella auténtica era magnifico!

My Version Of Ines's Paella De Marisco

Ingredients

- 6 cups clam or seafood broth
- 1 dozen mussels
- 12 large shrimp in shells
- 2 tbsp parsley
- 1 tbsp fresh thyme
- 8 tbsp olive oil
- 6 scallions, chopped
- 1 large tomato, chopped
- Lemon wedges

- 1 tsp thread saffron
- 1 dozen small clams
- Sea salt to taste
- 8 cloves garlic minced
- 2 tsp sweet smoked paprika
- 1 medium onion, chopped
- 1 red bell pepper, finely chopped
- 2 cups paella rice

Directions

01. Heat the broth in a large pot. Stir in saffron.

02. With a mortar and pestle mash parsley, garlic, thyme and ⅛ teaspoon salt into a paste.

03. Stir in paprika; add water if necessary to form a paste.

04. Heat 6 tablespoons of oil in 15 inch paella pan over medium high heat and quickly brown the fish 1 – 2 minutes. Do not fully cook.

05. Remove to warm platter.

06. Add remaining 2 tablespoons of oil, onion, scallions, and bell pepper to paella pan and cook until the vegetables are slightly softened.

07. Raise heat, add tomato, and cook until it becomes sauce-like, 2 – 5 minutes.

08. Pour in the hot broth and bring to a boil.

09. Sprinkle the rice evenly across the pan.

10. Boil for 3 minutes, stirring rice and rotating pan occasionally. Add all reserved fish (but not shrimp).

11. Stir in parsley paste. Taste for salt. Do not stir after this point.

12. Lower the heat and continue to simmer until rice is no longer soupy but enough liquid remains to continue cooking the rice (about 10 minutes). Add extra liquid if necessary.

13. Arrange shrimp, clams, and mussels over rice, placing edges of mussel and clam shells so they open facing up.

14. Cook, uncovered, for 15 – 20 minutes until rice is almost done.

15. Remove pan from heat and cover with foil. Let sit 10 minutes. Garnish with lemon wedges. Enjoy!

A Second **Serving**

Sharing the Gift of Food
from Family and Friends

"Memorable meals shared with family or friends is another page in the tapestry of your life to be treasured."

– Macawa

Many years ago, I sat in class at Cuyahoga Community College, Eastern Campus in Cleveland, Ohio. It was a computer class, but I didn't know how to even turn it on. I sat near and often partnered with a sweet, petite, studious, curly-haired woman who was about twenty years my senior. Her name was Mary Mele.

Mary explained that she wanted to learn more about computers. After working with her, I was certain she already knew lots more than I did. She told me she made programs for churches and other documents. We quickly became friends as we worked on group projects together. She was very patient, and when I become frustrated, she encouraged me.

That friendship and encouragement spanned over thirty-two years. Mary was a loving wife, mother, and grandmother; she was my strength when devastating illnesses ravaged my body, and when I lost my Mom in 1984, she was right by my side. She never forgot my birthday or important events involving my family. She often sent inspirational cards, and for each of my grandchildren's and children's births, she usually sent a memento. She and her husband Tony fed us, loved us, and made us a part of their extended family. I remember so many happy times we shared.

When we moved from Ohio to Georgia, I would go home each summer to visit family and friends. Although we were only there for a week, I always reserved a day to spend with Mary and her family. Her husband, Tony, manned the grill and she was "Princess of Sweet and Easy" treats. Her granddaughters who lived close by often joined us; we shared wonderful times and memories.

Each year she came up with another awesome dessert, and this memoir would be incomplete without at least a couple of them. We all looked forward to this annual event. When Mary and Tony happened to come visit friends in Villa Rica, Georgia, they would set aside time to spend with me and my family. Then, in mid 2015, sadly Mary lost a long, harrowing battle with dementia. She is sorely missed, yet each time I use one of her recipes I believe she is smiling down from heaven above.

Mary's Blueberry Delight

Ingredients

- *2 – 4 pints of blueberries (depending on how large the pan)
- ½ cups sugar
- 1 can of crushed pineapple
- ½ – 1 cup chopped pecans (optional)

- 1 box of butter recipe yellow cake mix
- 1 stick of butter
-

*(Frozen berries can also be used yielding 2 – 3 cups)

Directions

01. Spray a 9x13 inch baking dish lightly with cooking spray.

02. Pour blueberries into the pan and sprinkle sugar over them, then spread the crushed pineapple over them.

03. Next pour the dry cake mix over the fruit covering well.

04. Cut the stick of butter into small pieces and put on top of the dry cake mix. There will be areas that are still dry, but when the butter melts, it will spread.

05. If you like pecans, pour them over the top of everything.

06. Do not mix, just layer ingredients as instructed.

07. Place in a preheated 350 °F oven for 30 – 45 minutes or until the fruit is bubbly and a buttery crust is beginning to brown.

08. Handle it very carefully when you take it out from the oven.

It is very tasty on its own, or you can top with vanilla ice cream or whipped topping. If you use the frozen blueberries, prepare in the same manner. It will be a buttery, purple delight.

This is another delectable recipe among many others sent to me by Mary, who for years graced me with wonderful recipes and cookbooks. This will make one loaf; get a pot of your favorite coffee or tea to enjoy with this.

Mary's Orange Bread

Ingredients

- ¼ cup butter, softened
- 2 eggs beaten
- 2 cups flour
- 1 tsp baking powder
- Grated rind of one orange

- 1 cup sugar
- ⅔ cup buttermilk
- ½ tsp baking soda
- ¼ tsp salt
- 1 cup chopped nuts (optional)

Directions

01. Grease and flour a large loaf pan
02. Mix the ingredients together
03. Bake at 350 °F for 45 minutes to 1 hour.
04. When done, spoon over a topping made of juice of 1 orange and ½ cup sugar.
05. Let cool before cutting

Pig Pickin' Cake (Mandarin Orange Cake)

Wonderful refreshing fruit and cream goodness. A coworker of mine from a bank where I worked many years often made this cake for our office potluck lunches. Funny, she always said it was really an expensive and time-consuming cake to make, but not really and it is so good. Make sure you have room in the refrigerator to keep it cool since it has Cool Whip on it. I usually serve it for Easter and during summertime. Even for a novice, it is really easy to make.

Ingredients

- 1 (11 ounce) can mandarin oranges, ½ juice reserved

- 1 box yellow cake mix
- 4 eggs

- ¼ cup vegetable oil

Topping

- 1 (16 ounce) Package of frozen whipped topping, thawed

- 1 (15 ounce) Can crushed pineapple, drained

- 1 (3.5 ounce) Package of instant vanilla pudding mix

Directions

01. Preheat oven to 350 °F.

02. Grease and flour three 8 inch round cake pans.

03. Mix together cake mix, canned oranges, juice, eggs, and oil. Pour batter into pans. (layers will be thin.)

04. Bake 22 – 28 minutes, then test for doneness.

05. When done, let pan cool on wire rack for about 10 minutes, then remove from pan and cool on wire rack.

06. Prepare topping by mixing together all ingredients, then spread on a completely cooled cake, between layers, on sides and top.

07. Refrigerate until ready to serve.

Get ready to watch your family and guests make lil pigs out of themselves, it is that good!

Jazzy's Key Lime Cake

Jazzmin—dazzling smile, big heart, with a love for the best foods imaginable. We worked together, studied together, traveled together, and noshed on great foods together. While I was studying journalism at Georgia Perimeter College, she often bought me delectable and nutritious meals... she knew how focused I was. I would not stop studying or doing classwork to eat.

One day while I was struggling to solve an algebra problem outside the math lab, she arrived, pushed a sandwich in front of me, and said "Eat!" She shoved a bottle of cold peach tea in my direction and sat down, unpacking her computer and books. I bit into the brown, soft bread... my taste buds cried, "More, more!" The sandwich was dressed with lime-flavored mayonnaise, bean sprouts, slices of tomato and creamy avocado, thin cool cucumber slices, slivers of onion, and a veggie-based cheese slice. The different tastes and textures were an explosion of wonderful in my mouth.

She taught me how to be an unabashed foodie and to feed my "inner fat girl." While serving in student government, we traveled to New York city for an APCA conference. There she and her father, Harry Hunter, who lived in New York, introduced me to Katz's Deli, and my life has never been the same. Ahhh a true New York deli, like none that I had ever visited. I still have dreams of the tender, thick, juicy slabs of hand-cut pastrami and corned beef.

Fast forward... we have spent many Thursday evenings enjoying tasty salads that consisted of cool, crisp cucumbers, sweet tomatoes, and creamy avocado tossed in olive oil and lemon or lime juice; coconut chicken or shrimp; warm, toasty, crusty, buttered Cuban bread; cool, fruity, sweet red Easy Muscadine; and various sparkling wines as we watched our favorite T.G.I.T. line-up on the television.

Jazzmin also taught me the joys of Spanish café con leche and perusing Trader Joe's for wonderful and unique foods. She was responsible for introducing me to many types of international cuisine, as well as baking amazing cakes. I would be remiss if I didn't include a recipe she shared with me that I have shared with key lime lovers.

Ingredients

- 1 (18.25 ounce) package lemon cake mix

- 1 can of Comstock Cherry filling (the one with extra cherries).

- 1 (3 ounce) pack lime flavored gelatin mix

- 1½ cups vegetable oil
- 4 eggs

- ¾ cup orange juice

Icing

- ½ cup butter
- 1 (8 ounce) package cream cheese

- 3 tbsp fresh lime juice
- 4 cups confectioners' sugar

- Add a little key lime juice to the icing while mixing it to give it a little extra kick.

Directions

01. Combine cake mix, gelatin mix, oil, eggs, and orange juice.

02. Pour into three 8 inch cake pans. Bake according to instructions on box. Allow to cool.

03. Spread the cherry filling between the layers, reserving a little to decorate the top with.

04. To make the frosting: In a large bowl, beat the butter and cream cheese until light and fluffy. Add lime juice and confectioners' sugar. Mix well and Spread over cooled cake.

Sister Bate's Dump Cake

My children and I attended a wonderful little church in Scottdale, Georgia, in the early 1990s: All Nations Church of God, which has been blessed to grow tremendously into All Nations Life and Praise Cathedral and relocated to Stockbridge, Georgia. You could always go there for a true word from God, Bible-based teaching, phenomenal praise and worship, and some of the best cooking I ever tasted. There were many capable cooks who shared their talents, including Southern fried chicken, macaroni and cheese, and the best banana pudding ever. Sis Shields and her sisters could make rocks taste good.

I was then introduced to a dessert that has become a family favorite: Sister Bate's dump cake. Not only could she sing the hell out of you, she could cook! My son Jermael and baby brother Vernon could eat the entire pan, it was that good to them.

I took this to school to share with my classmates, and they loved it.

Just like the name says, you just dump the ingredients into the pan and let the oven work it out. Not only could she sing the hell out of you, she could cook! This recipe is probably not exactly the same as hers was, but it's the next best thing to it. It is so easy and tastes rich and fruity. I like to enjoy it warm with vanilla ice cream on top.

Ingredients

- 1 box of butter recipe yellow cake mix
- 1 can of crushed pineapple
- 1½ stick of butter (or more if you like)
- 2 cans of cherry pie filling (not tart)
- ¾ cup sugar

Directions

01. Preheat oven to 350 °F.

02. Spray a Bundt cake pan with nonstick spray.

03. Dump one can of cherries into the pan (shaking pan to level it out after each addition of fruit), and sprinkle half of the sugar over it.

04. Dump in crushed pineapples, do not drain juice.

05. Dump in the other can of cherry pie filling. Sprinkle remaining sugar over them.

06. Dump dry cake mix over the fruit, covering completely.

07. Cut the butter in small pieces and dot all over the top of the dry cake mix.

08. Bake in oven for 35 – 45 minutes, until the buttery crust is golden brown.

Bon appétit!

Peach Blueberry Cobbler

I love fruits, I love cobblers, so this is a dessert that I came up with that combined my favorite fruits and my school (Agnes Scott College) color—purple. The fruit excites your taste buds and the crust makes you want more. If you are not a fan of blueberries, you can omit them, and it will be a tasty peach cobbler.

Batter

- ½ cup melted butter
- 1 cup sugar
- ¼ tsp salt
- 1 room-temperature egg
- 1 cup flour
- 2 tsp baking powder
- ⅔ cup room temperature milk

Filling

- 1 (28 ounce) can sliced peaches, drained
- 1 Pint of fresh blueberries
- 1 cup sugar
- ½ tsp nutmeg
- 1 tsp cinnamon

Directions

01. Melt butter in a 9x13 inch pan

02. Mix together flour, sugar, baking powder, & salt

03. Stir in milk & egg

04. Pour evenly over melted butter

05. Combine peaches, sugar, & spices, then gently toss in blueberries

06. Spread over batter—DO NOT STIR!

07. Bake 35 – 45 minutes at 350 °F until batter comes to the top and is golden brown

08. Serve warm with ice cream

Myesha's Grape Salad

When my sons were attending LaGrange College, I often visited the campus and met many wonderful staff members, students, and their families. My youngest son was the running back for the newly formed football team and looked forward to our Saturdays on "the hill." We parents often shared recipes, foods, and our love for football.

Of the many foods I experienced, one that really stood out was the grape salad. My daughter Myesha mastered this delicious treat for our family to enjoy. It was cool, sweet, delicious, and easy to make.

Buy grapes, either red or white; seedless is best. Take them off the stems and wash them. Let them dry thoroughly or the creamy stuff won't stick to them.

In a bowl, mix one softened block of cream cheese and one medium container of sour cream. Mix in ⅓ cup of sugar and a teaspoon of vanilla. Mix in the grapes gently.

I put the mixture in a flat pan, that way there is more surface for the topping. The topping is simply sprinkled brown sugar and then granola cereal without raisins (Kellogg's low-fat granola or something similar).

Put in the fridge for a few hours to let it firm up. That's it.

Lucky's Zucchini Bread

I decided to visit my youngest sister, Lucky, and her family in Mobile, Alabama, for Easter. I think holidays are best served with family and friends. I often celebrated with my own children and grandchildren but decided to do something different. I had a darling little grand-niece there in Mobile whom I had never met.

My sister has always been a wonderful hostess: she gladly takes you to places of interest, through the downtown area. We enjoyed a wonderful play, Aida, at the amazing Joe Johnson Playhouse one evening, and we visited the colorful "Art and Design of Mardi Gras" exhibition at the Mobile Museum of Art. It was a beautiful sunny spring day, and my sister, her daughter Danyalle, and Danyalle's little girl Leslee enjoyed the sights and history displayed.

Once we returned to Lucky's home, I quickly went into her kitchen and retrieved a slice of heaven that she had baked earlier: her moist and delicious Zucchini bread. And all this time I had only roasted, smothered with onions, or tossed in salads this crisp, green vegetable. I am certain that even if zucchini causes you to scrunch up your nose, if you try this recipe, your opinion will be changed—for the better. Grab a cup of coffee, your favorite tea, or a glass of milk and tickle your taste buds. Delicious!

Ingredients

- 3 cups all-purpose flour
- 1 tsp baking soda
- 3 tsp ground cinnamon
- 1 cup vegetable oil
- 3 tsp vanilla extract
- 1 cup chopped walnuts

- 1 tsp salt
- 1 tsp baking powder
- 3 eggs
- 2¼ cups white sugar
- 2 cups grated zucchini

Directions

01. Preheat oven to 325 °F.

02. Grease and flour two 8x4 inch pans.

03. Sift flour, salt, baking powder, soda, and cinnamon together in a bowl.

04. Cream eggs, oil, vanilla, and sugar together in a large bowl.

05. Add sifted ingredients to the creamed mixture and beat well.

06. Stir in zucchini and nuts until well combined. Pour batter into prepared pans.

07. Bake for 40 to 60 minutes, or until tester inserted in the center comes out clean.

08. Cool in pan on rack for 20 minutes. Remove bread from pan and completely cool.

09. If there are any leftovers, you can place in the refrigerator or even freeze a loaf for later.

Auntie Carolyn's Yeast Rolls — Roll With It, Babe!

I met Carolyn more than forty years ago, when we were young, cute, sexy, and sweet. We started attending Cuyahoga Community College in the '70s and were roommates. We loved to go dancing, and occasionally we enjoyed a wine cocktail (don't judge, wine has been around since biblical times) at Champion City Elks Club on East 55th in Cleveland.

Carolyn was like another mother to my children and a sincere and close friend. She was always amazing; after I lost my mom, she scooped me up after the funeral and took me to Bloomington, Illinois, to attend the Passion Play. This was after she had helped me every step of the way in preparing for my mother's funeral services. She taught my oldest sons how to love stuff that I couldn't imagine cooking, like Malt-o-Meal, Cream of Wheat... yeeeach. To each his or her own. We have laughed, cried, sewed clothing for ourselves and others—she is a woman of many talents (she is also an amazing seamstress, at one time working for Fisher body, sewing seat covers).

We have also prayed together—she is a strong woman of God, and her son, my awesome minister of music nephew Frank, also benefited from a strong spiritual foundation as well as his mother's mouth-watering cooking abilities. Trust me when I tell you that Carolyn makes a pound cake so delectable that it is indescribable.

Ingredients

- ½ cup warm water
- 2 tbsp sugar
- 1 pound butter (softened)
- 8 cups or more flour*
- 2 tbsp salt

- 2 cakes yeast (packages of dry)
- 2 cups cold milk
- ¾ cup sugar
- 4 eggs

Note: Dough can be frozen before first rise

Directions

01. Dissolve yeast and 2 tablespoons sugar in ½ cup warm water. Let stand until yeast bubbles.

02. Add butter, milk, eggs, and sugar. Cream.

03. Add flour and salt (mix salt into flour, no need to sift) 1 cup at a time. Mix dough until as stiff or smooth as desired. *Must use 8 cups of flour

04. Form into a ball, place in bowl, and cover with a towel until dough has doubled in size.

05. Punch dough and form into balls (using flour on hands to keep dough from sticking) at the size of golf balls; flatten and fold in half.

06. Place on cookie sheets, cover with towel. Let rise until rolls have doubled in size.

07. Bake for 10 – 12 minutes at 350 °F. Should make about 6 dozen rolls.

Enjoy! I certainly did.

My Quick And Easy Lasagna

Sometimes you want something hearty, delicious, and comforting. This lasagna is easy to prepare, too. Great for gatherings. Quick and easy, it tastes like it took hours to make!

Ingredients

- 1 box of no boil lasagna noodles (1 box per pan that you are making)

- About 2 pounds of ground turkey or beef

- Garlic powder, salt and pepper to taste

- 2 tbsp Worcestershire sauce

- 1 tsp Oregano

- 1 tsp Basil

- 2 jars of your favorite spaghetti sauce; I used tomato & basil, or mushroom, or garlic, whatever you prefer.

- Cottage cheese (the larger size carton with 2 eggs beaten into it) or Ricotta cheese

- Mozzarella, Colby-jack, sharp cheddar, and/or the assorted shredded Italian cheese blends (I use 3 different cheeses, one 8-oz bag of each). The more you use the cheesier it is. (Reserve a little of the sharp cheese to put on the top.)

Directions

01. Put 1 tablespoon of sugar into each jar of sauce and mix well; this will decrease the chance of getting indigestion from the tomato sauce.

02. There are instructions on the box of lasagna you can also use as a guide. DO NOT BOIL.

03. Brown the meat, and sprinkle Worcestershire sauce in it while cooking.

04. Add seasonings as well: salt, pepper, garlic powder, oregano, basil.

05. Pour enough sauce to cover the bottom of the pan (a thin layer—also add a little water to thin it out a little), then put a layer of the uncooked dry lasagna, then drain the cooked meat and add some of the tomato sauce to it.

06. Put a layer of the meat on the noodles, then top with of the some shredded cheese (just sprinkle some of all of the bags of cheese over the meat, kinda mix them up).

07. Top with another layer of noodles, then meat, then the cottage cheese mixture, then another layer of noodles, then meat, then cheese.

08. After putting on your top layer of noodles, pour some sauce over it and sprinkle cheese over it.

09. Cover it with foil and bake for 50 minutes.

10. Remove foil and bake for 5 minutes more. Then enjoy it.

This seems complicated but it is really easy as soon as you get started.

Martha's Mmmmm Macaroni And Cheese

One of my most requested items to prepare is my macaroni and cheese, which was inspired by several close friends. I just observed them over the years, and by the processes of addition and subtraction, used what I felt made it amazingly mouth-watering and continually tweaked and revised it until it was what I wanted mine to be.

Ingredients

- 2 cups extra sharp cheese
- 1 cup medium cheddar cheese
- 1 cup Colby-Jack cheese (Co-jack)
- 1 can evaporated milk
- 16-ounce box of elbow macaroni boiled in lightly salted water with 1 tsp olive oil in it.
- ¾ package of cream cheese, room temp, cut into little cubes (I either buy shredded or shred my cheeses)
- Add one cup of your favorite cheese—some people like to use Velveeta
- ½ cup of milk to beat eggs into before adding to hot pasta; this will prevent eggs from scrambling.

I try to have 6 – 7 different cheeses in it. Reserve some sharp cheddar to sprinkle over the top before popping it into the oven.

I also add ¼ of a diced sweet onion in it with the cheeses, really makes them tastier.

Directions

01. Mix into drained hot macaroni ½ stick of butter and cream cheese till starting to blend. Then add in other cheeses.

02. Add 2 teaspoons dried mustard, ¼ teaspoon cayenne pepper, ½ teaspoon black pepper.

03. Moisten with 1 can of evaporated milk.

04. Cheeses should be melting and blending.

05. Add salt to taste.

06. Beat 2 eggs into ½ cup milk; after well beaten, pour into the mixture, then mix and pour into casserole dish.

07. Sprinkle sharp cheddar on top and place in 360 °F oven for 25 minutes or until cheese is bubbling and starting to brown.

Enjoy! Tell me how you like it.

Martha's Savory Horseradish-Crusted Rib Roast

This was my dinner for New Year's Dinner 2010. It was not only delectable, it was also a visual delight. I wanted to start the new year with a totally new attitude, as I was about to return to school after being out of school for over thirty years. This was the first time I had attempted to make it.

Ingredients

- 1 small bag of baby carrots (rinsed)
- 6 – 8 celery ribs (rinsed)
- 3 tbsp olive oil
- 1 beef standing rib roast (4 – 5 pounds)
- ¾ cups horseradish sauce
- ¼ tbsp pepper (or less depending on your taste, grinding peppercorn is good too)

- 8 – 10 baby or new redskin potatoes
- 1 large sweet onion
- 3 sprigs fresh rosemary (rinsed)
- 1 tbsp kosher salt (or less if desired)
- 1½ tbsp Worcestershire sauce
- Fresh mushrooms (optional)

Directions

01. Preheat oven to 475 °F.

02. Slice baby carrots long way in half or close to it. Slice small potatoes about 1½ to 2 inches thick so they will be circular like potato chips. Slice onion and celery into 1-inch pieces.

03. Combine veggies in large bowl with olive oil; stir until they are coated with oil.

04. Transfer onto lightly oiled roasting pan (except for mushrooms).

05. Season roast on all sides with salt, I love fresh garlic so I made a few small slits in roast and inserted slivers in them.

06. Place roast on rack arranged over veggies (wash hands!).

07. Place roast in oven and immediately reduce heat to 325 °F, bake for one hour.

08. Meanwhile remove rosemary leaves from stems, chop finely, combine in bowl with horseradish sauce, Worcestershire sauce, and pepper. Set aside.

09. After an hour is up, remove roast from oven, coat with horseradish mixture.

10. Return roast to oven, bake 1½ to 2 more hours or until meat thermometer reaches 145 °F (medium rare) up to 170 °F (well done). My veggies had roasted nicely so I removed them and placed mushrooms in bottom of pan in drippings.

11. Use a meat thermometer to ensure degree of doneness.

12. Transfer roast to cutting board when done and let it rest about 10 – 15 minutes before cutting.

Kevin's Red Hot Sticky Wings

My son Kevin loves chicken wings, fried, baked, or grilled. Kevin has combined a number of seasonings to make rubs to marinate his wings in prior to grilling. He has shown me how to use many different spices to make them as unique and tasty as they can be. Dry rubs, hot rubs, spicy rubs... be creative!

This is a selection of some of Kevin's wonderful wing recipes—they are so yummy.

Ingredients

- 1½ pounds chicken wings, cut at joints and wing tips removed
- House Seasoning, recipe follows
- 1 tbsp minced garlic
- ½ cup tangy, red barbecue sauce
- ¼ cup honey
- 1 tsp crushed red pepper flakes, optional
- 1 tbsp vegetable oil
- 2 tbsp hot sauce
- 2 tbsp butter
- Peanut oil, for frying
- Celery sticks and red bell pepper slices, for serving

Seasoning

- 1 cup salt
- ¼ cup garlic powder
- ¼ cup black pepper

Mix ingredients together and store in an airtight container for up to six months.

Directions

01. Preheat oven to 400 °F.

02. Lay the chicken wings out in a single layer on a rimmed baking sheet and season with House Seasoning.

03. Bake for 20 minutes.

04. Sauté the garlic in vegetable oil in a medium saucepan over medium-low heat until softened and fragrant. Stir in sweet barbecue sauce, hot sauce, and honey.

05. Bring to a boil, then lower and simmer for 15 minutes until thick. If using crushed red pepper flakes, add and cook 30 seconds more.

06. Stir in butter until melted and smooth. Pour into a large mixing bowl.

07. Heat oil in a deep-fryer or large Dutch oven to 350 °F.

08. Fry the baked wings for 10 minutes until golden and crisp. Transfer to a paper-towel-lined sheet pan to drain.

09. Toss the fried wings in the red sauce to coat.

10. Transfer to a platter and serve with celery sticks, carrots, and red bell pepper slices.

Blue Cheese Dipping Sauce

Ingredients

- 1 cup crumbled blue cheese
- ¼ cup mayonnaise
- 1 tsp fresh lemon juice
- ½ tsp salt
- ¼ cup sour cream
- ½ cup buttermilk
- ½ tsp minced garlic
- Freshly ground black pepper

Directions

01. Combine all ingredients in a small bowl and stir to combine.

02. Serve immediately or store, covered and refrigerated, for up to one week before serving.

03. Sauce may be made thicker by mashing some of the crumbled blue cheese against the side of the bowl. Sauce is better if allowed to sit for one or two days before serving. Fresh is delicious!

Bourbon Street Buffalo Wings

Ingredients for the sauce

- 2 tbsp butter
- 1 large shallot, chopped
- 2 garlic cloves, chopped
- 2 ounces bourbon
- ½ cup brown sugar
- ½ cup honey
- 8 ounces barbecue sauce
- 8 ounces chili sauce
- 1 tbsp ancho pepper, finely chopped
- 3 ounces wing sauce

Ingredients for the wings

- Oil, for frying
- 50 chicken wings
- Blue cheese dressing, for serving
- Bourbon, for serving

Directions for the sauce

01. In a large saucepan, melt the butter.

02. Add the shallot and garlic cloves and sauté, about two to three minutes.

03. Stir in the bourbon, brown sugar, and honey to heat through, one minute.

04. Next add the ancho pepper, chili sauce, barbecue sauce, and wing sauce and cook, stirring occasionally for two minutes. Keep warm until ready to serve.

Directions for the chicken wings

01. Heat oil in a deep-fryer.

02. As you make the sauce, drop chicken wings, in batches (the amount you drop in at 1 time will depend on the size of your fryer) into the deep-fryer.

03. Fry until golden brown on both sides. Remove the wings from the oil and drain.

04. Add the wings to a large mixing bowl and toss in the sauce, coating each wing.

05. Serve blue cheese dressing and ½ shots of bourbon, on the side, for adults to sip.

Baked Honey Sesame Wings

Ingredients

- ¼ cup honey
- ⅓ cup water
- 2 tbsp sesame oil
- 3 scallions, sliced
- 2 tbsp sesame seeds
- ½ cup low-sodium soy sauce
- ¼ cup hoisin sauce
- 2½ – 3 lbs. chicken wings
- 2 garlic cloves, minced
- Pinch of salt
- 1 tbsp sriracha sauce (add more to taste if you like)

Directions

01. Preheat oven to 400 °F.

02. In large bowl or plastic bag, combine all the ingredients, except the chicken, and mix well.

03. Add chicken to the marinade and cover.

04. Marinate in refrigerator for one hour or up to three hours.

05. Remove wings from marinade when finished and place on a lined baking sheet.

06. Bake for 30 minutes at 400 °F.

07. Top with sesame seeds and scallions before serving, if desired.

Baked Hot Wings

My oldest son, Brian, and godson Ant often made the tastiest fried hot wings that I had ever wrapped my lips around. In an effort to eat a little healthier, this is my baked version.

Ingredients

- 2 tsp cayenne pepper
- ½ tsp onion powder
- 20 Chicken wings
- ½ cup hot pepper sauce, such as Frank's Red Hot
- ½ tsp garlic powder
- ½ tsp salt
- ½ cup melted butter

Don't be afraid to try new flavors, add jerk seasoning, or brown sugar and spice rub for wings for variety.

Directions

01. Line a baking sheet with aluminum foil, and lightly grease with cooking spray.

02. After washing and draining wings, sprinkle with seasoning.

03. Place the wings onto the prepared baking sheet, and place into the refrigerator. Refrigerate at least one hour.

04. Preheat oven to 400 °F.

05. Bake in the preheated oven until the chicken is no longer pink in the center, and crispy on the outside, about 45 minutes. Turn the wings over halfway during cooking so they cook evenly.

06. Whisk together the melted butter and hot sauce in a small bowl. Toss the wings into the sauce mixture, and enjoy with fresh veggies.

Final **Thoughts**

It Had to Start Somewhere:
Sharing the Comforts of Food and Memories

"Food is not rational. Food is culture, habit, craving, and identity."

– Jonathan Safran Foer

Excited about my senior year of college and upcoming senior project, I considered what I could write that would uniquely represent me. I thought of trying to weave together some special memories that would touch generations, and I decided to write a food memoir. Sure, I could write poems or stories, but a food memoir would represent not only me, but also those whose shoulders I stood upon to get to that point.

I began the summer by compiling a reading list of food memoirs that had been recommended to me. Then I began researching, browsing, and finally reading. Reading the varied collection of food memoirs over the summer brought back to my re-memories family times shared with my grandparents and other family members. They had migrated from the South to the Midwest in search of a better life. Did they find it? In some cases, they just found life.

I remembered that holidays, comfort foods, and family togetherness were very important to my family. We would all collectively contribute to the feasts, preparing delicious foods that would nourish both the body and the soul. Face-to-face, precious family time. Through my families' nurturing and cooking, they shared with us what they could not always say aloud. Silently and deliciously they shared love, hope, memories, and cultural continuity. But sadly, whenever one of our family members died, special memories and recipes were forever lost to us. What better time than the present to start collecting those gems to be shared for generations to come?

To prepare I began to read a variety of recommended food memoirs from notable authors. I picked up Laurie Colwin's Home Cooking from the county library. It was filled with advice as well as recipes. Happily I curled up with the amazing memoir, filled with life, insight, wit, common sense, and mouthwatering descriptions.

On several occasions I was enticed to race to the market, buy the ingredients, and try to make the dish that was described. I gathered fresh and tasty vegetables and herbs to prepare: curly green kale, firm Brussels sprouts, radiant red and golden peppers, as well as fragrant rosemary and basil. Delightful!

More often than not I was successful in duplicating the delectability of the dish. I was excited and intrigued, and ideas sometimes flowed from my mind like water from a spring. I tucked *Home Cooking* close and read it at every opportunity of free time, even totally isolating myself, happily curled up reading the book on the weekend.

I imagined being in Laurie Colwin's large, well-equipped kitchen, with the latest amenities. All the while, looking out of the window into a garden filled with organic vegetables, ripe and colorful, along with fresh, fragrant herbs—I was captivated. Page after page I felt as if I were perched on a stool on Colwin's kitchen, watching her create her epicurean delights. I could imagine that I could smell it, taste it.

I even enhanced a recipe that she shared for oven-cooked ribs. Sticky, flavorful, tender, fingertip-sucking good. To accompany my ribs I gathered fresh veggies: colorful peppers, yellow squash, zucchini, mushrooms, tender asparagus, and slices of eggplant. I drizzled olive oil over them, threw in a little garlic, and popped them in the oven (350 °F for about 20 minutes more or less, until they were tender). Yumm!

Initially Colwin affected the way I looked at preparing foods, in a way different from what I normally had. More important, she showed me how to bring my reader into my kitchen, to smell, taste, and experience my joy at cooking the meal through reading my words. In just five sittings I had completed Colwin's book, which for me ended too soon, yet was comparable to what I imagined relishing a meal at a Michelin starred restaurant would be like.

I reached into my summer book reading box and pulled out another selection, *Tender at the Bone,* by Ruth Reichl. Finding a cozy, comfy bench where the sun bronzed my shoulders and a breeze brushed my cheeks, I again curled up with another book that left me wanting more. I was intrigued at how she wove painful and poignant re-memories like her mother's mental illness into the story, or her father's illness and subsequent death. She was not seeking sympathy but was taking charge of her life, which probably saved her sanity. She dealt with life while creating recipes that made me ravenous—hungry for cheeses, wines, and other special dishes. At times I had a glass of sweet red or Muscadine wine while reading or a fruitful sangria close by with a side of apple slices, cheese, and crackers. I completed the memoir quickly, learning other methods of making my writing appealing to my readers.

Then I picked up _A Homemade Life_ by the delightful Molly Wizenberg. She made me want to duplicate her prunes with citrus and cinnamon, especially when I was in Madrid and they had fruit compote on the breakfast buffet. When I tried it, I believed that the pages of her book had come to life. During this time, my process included reading and researching various types of food memoirs. This enabled me to see the differences in the ways they were written. It also helped me to understand and discover ways to compose my food memoir, distinguishing it from being just a cookbook.

Just as I was getting into the book, my son Kevin drove me to Ohio to visit two special women in my life who were battling cancer. He felt that I needed this trip before I left the country. He is wise beyond his years.

One woman succumbed two days after I was able to sit, talk to, and pray with her. She was nearly ninety and had touched many lives. R.I. H Dean, also known as Granny.

I had gone to school with the other woman I visited. She had lost her two sisters and mom to cancer and recently had been diagnosed with throat cancer. She was terrified. Chemo and radiation were grueling. I needed to reassure her before I left for Spain. It was a bittersweet reunion, as her sister had passed two weeks earlier. We needed that moment, that day. I told her she would survive, I hugged her, and we cried and prayed together. She even came from Cleveland the following year for my college graduation. Unfortunately she succumbed to cancer two years later. That final year we were closer than ever and spent as much time as possible together, but that is another story.

In addition to seeing family and friends, my son Kevin and I also sampled some of our Midwestern favorites: corned beef sandwiches, washed down by ice cold beer. Kevin and I returned to Georgia, and I continued to prepare for my trip to Spain.

On my flight to Europe, I pulled out *A Homemade Life* again—I had eight hours to kill. As I read it, I felt that I was following Wizenberg from room to room, taste to taste. I knew that I must try some of her recipes, like her cauliflower tinted with turmeric. I have learned much more about spices and herbs that I had never considered trying. She made me dare to be adventurous when using them.

I discovered that not only was hers a memoir of touching memories and superb menus, it was also about life, losses, and love. I was able to visualize the places she traveled and the dishes she prepared and ate during her travels. I also realized that, like Wizenberg, my writing would be more powerful when I shared recipes, as well as nostalgic memories. It was okay to include poignant stories about my life. I smiled as she described Brandon's (who she eventually married) vinegar needs, and I thought of my five-year-old grandson who insists on vinegar on his greens and salads, and my youngest son Mario's need for olives, pickled okra, and other vinegary, pickled and salty veggies. I had introduced Mario to them while catering events and putting together relish trays; he was then about seven, and years later it is still with him.

Molly's story was rich with life, love, and adventure. It was gentle and filling like a favorite comfort food.

On a beautiful day in mid-June, I embarked on an amazing adventure and opportunity. I traveled to Spain to study and totally immerse myself in the culture. I was fortunate to be selected as a participant in this global awareness opportunity. Madrid was my destination for the first week, and then I travelled north to Oviedo, Spain. For four weeks I attended the University of Oviedo. The total immersion into the Spanish culture and community made my textbooks come to life. I rode on a crazy fast train, in excess of 200 kilometers per hour. During my stay I resided with a host family. I also visited markets, museums, cathedrals, and other notable places of interest. I also collected recipes in addition to pictures to share with my family and friends when I returned. I couldn't think of a better way of bringing a taste of my experience into my memoir.

My next offering was *Best Food Writing 2013*, edited by Holly Hughes. I flipped through the titles that were listed and decided I probably wasn't going to have time to read the entire book, so I looked for titles that aroused my curiosity. While living with my host "sister" in Oviedo, I was energized after my daily *siesta* and would often go outdoors with the book in my hand. I assumed that this anthology of sorts would give me an interesting and varied selection of essays to read. There were lots of peaceful and beautiful parks, one of which was behind the building I lived in. I went to the park on many sunny afternoons to enjoy the weather and the amazing views, and squeezed in a little reading.

The good little girl in me started with the very first offering of the book. I discovered the delights of Brett Martin's essay, *"Good Food Everywhere,"* in which he travels, tastes, critiques, enjoys, and sometimes abhors certain foods he is offered. I discovered that there really is the oddly named Momofuku Milk Bar. I think it would be wonderful to have a discriminating palate and travel across the lands, off the popular paths, to sample dishes at local eateries. His descriptions of certain dishes elicited gasps of deprivation from the depths of my stomach. I was intrigued by Martin's take on Rex Hospital, the "Rex Carlton." A hospital that cares about the health, nutrition, and true taste of foods—now that is total customer-focused care.

I followed that up by reading *"Cooking Isn't Fun"* by Tracie McMillan. It was a quite informative essay that reinforced my reasoning and love for cooking from scratch, loving the aromas that jolt my senses. I cannot think of anything that compares with the wonderful smell of fresh garlic and onions sweating in oil on the stove, or the comforting aroma of a tender-to-the-bone, slow-cooked roast nestled among carrots, celery, potatoes, and slivers of colorful bell peppers, splashed with Worcestershire sauce. Yes! Or the way my marinated sautéed kale turns a vibrant shade of green, holding its form and flavor, as its fragrance dances throughout my kitchen.

On the other hand it was gory (to me) reading the details of the making of *morcilla*, blood sausage, from *Hogonomics*, a selection by Barry Estabrook. The essays dipped into

Farm to Table, Home Cooking, and wound into *The Meat of the Matter*, ending appropriately in *Personal Tastes,* and most were amazing reads.

Julia Child ushered me into a time machine that took me back, back to the years 1949–1960 and spirited me away to Paris and her maiden voyage in France and French cuisine. *My Life in France* was simply captivating. She led me through wineries, fine restaurants, sea shores, and scenic landscapes that only Europe could provide. She placed me in the midst of times and places of turmoil—the Cold War, McCarthyism, and unrest in Europe. But she also included me in the story of her life and love of her husband and Paris; it was quite a sojourn. It confirmed that I could effectively include food and travel in my memoir.

"We are blessed since we can find our ovens and stoves and make up for some of what we long for."

– Ntozake Shange

Summer break was winding down and I continued to grapple with what to include in, or exclude from, this food memoir. I quieted my mind and listened to melodic spiritual flutes, guitars, and meditations from far shores. I then picked up a late suggestion to my reading list, *If I Can Cook, You Know God Can* by Ntozake Shange. I was slightly familiar with the author but not with this memoir. It was described as a "soul nourishing cookbook." The book shared tasty and eclectic recipes that are tidbits of cultures: culinary delicacies, a bit of history, ageless vernacular, and philosophy. It told stories of resilience, revolutions, and recipes.

Finally back in school, I reevaluated my decision to write a food memoir, and I decided it was a good fit for me. I'd received numerous urgings and encouraging words from family and friends. "Yes you must do it, please write it, I want to read it!" they said. Their encouragement was the booster I needed. With journals spread near and my computers within fingertip reach, I wrote, recreated, recollected.

"Food is not just food."

– *Stacia Ashe*

One day I was talking to a new student about my project as we walked around campus. I ran into her a few days later. She hugged me and excitedly told me that she had something for me. She reached into her bag and brought out a blue book titled *The Best of Life is At the Table*, and it had pictures of foods and a spoon and fork. I opened it and found it was a journal with wonderful inspirational quotes scattered throughout. She told me that when she saw it, she knew it would be perfect to jot down notes for my food memoir. What a nice surprise. I love it, and yes I use it.

A month into the semester someone recommended that I look at *Hallelujah*, the Welcome Table: Lifetime of Memories W/ Recipes by Maya Angelou. I had been so immersed in my studies that I was unaware she had written this book. It was good reading, but intimidating for a novice like myself. I began to question myself: are my essays too long? My astute English department advisor immediately noticed a difference in my writing. "No, don't hold back, keep writing as you were doing," she encouraged me. She explained that Angelou's Hallelujah was more of a cookbook than a memoir.

For several months I had been filling my journals with thoughts about how to write the memoir, which recipes to include, and what memories to share. I have rethought and revised ideas at each step of creating this work. Will everyone be as eager to read the truths as I recall them about growing up? Maybe, maybe not. I have found satisfaction sifting through piles of collected memories and recipes and re-visualizing their connections. Revisiting those places and times tucked safely inside sometimes caused bittersweet memories that I have never before spoken about. Surprisingly it was at times poignant yet cathartic. But it also showed inner strength and contentment.

I have incorporated some of those delightful and interesting moments from the heart into my memoir. Like wildflowers in a field, they were colorful and multifarious. I found many amazing instances of cooking, cultures, traditions, and family in the various books I read. I discovered the importance of seeking and sharing those family recipes, and continuing the traditions that should be timeless.

I have found how to show, more than tell, of my experiences; my readers should be able to imagine the dinner table just as I experienced it. Yes there are emotions tied to these meals. But food is more than just food—it's life giving, memory evoking. My essays are based on certain foods and experiences throughout my life.

My initial thought of a food memoir was that it was a collection of recipes with the stories that made them memorable. Usually when someone shares a recipe with you, they also share a story connected with it. Poignant and sometimes painful memories, many that I had never shared, have found their way from deep in my heart. Distinctly important times in my life that I decided to incorporate into my memoir were reawakened on these pages.

My goal has been to engage my reader and introduce them to some wonderful dishes to add to their own collection of recipes. I hope to leave my readers hungering for more, salivating for a taste of a dish, a time, a place, or a tradition. Maybe I will encourage dialogue among families and friends, to share recipes and memories that will be passed along through future generations. It has to start somewhere.

Works Cited

01. Angelou, Maya. Hallelujah! The Welcome Table. New York: Random House, 2004. Print.

02. Child, Julia, and Alex Prud'homme. *My Life in France.* New York: Alfred A. Knopf, 2006. Print.

03. Colwin, Laurie. *Home Cooking.* New York: Knopf, 1988. Print.

04. David, Elizabeth. *An Omelette and a Glass of Wine.* New York, NY, U.S.A.: Viking, 1985. Print.

05. Hughes, Holly. *Best Food Writing 2013.* N.p.: n.p., n.d. Print.

06. Reichl, Ruth. *Tender at the Bone: Growing Up at the Table.* New York: Random House, 1998. Print.

07. Shange, Ntozake. *If I Can Cook, You Know God Can.* Boston: Beacon, 1998. Print.

08. Wizenberg, Molly. *A Homemade Life: Stories and Recipes from My Kitchen Table.* New York: Simon & Schuster, 2009. Print.

Made in the USA
Columbia, SC
12 July 2020